Blogging:
A 6-Figure Strategy

Thomas Benson

Copyright © 2019 by Thomas Benson

All rights reserved. No part of this book may be used or reproduced by any means, graphic, electronic, or mechanical, including photocopying, recording, taping, or by any information storage retrieval system, without the written permission of the publisher except in the case of brief quotations embodied in critical articles and reviews.

WEST SUSSEX LIBRARY SERVICE	
202120373	
Askews & Holts	02-Mar-2022
658.872	

Contents

Introduction 1

Chapter 1: How to Start a Blog? 3

Chapter 2: Niche 10

Chapter 3: Domains and hosting 23

Chapter 4: Types of Blogs 33

Chapter 5: Getting Started with Writing a New Blog 39

Chapter 6: Optimizing Your Blog For SEO 60

Chapter 7: Focus on Growing Your Audience 70
    Look Beyond Your Website 70
    Build an Online Presence 72
    Seek to Network with Others 75
    Consider Paid Promotions 77

Chapter 8: Monetize Through Sponsored Content 80

Chapter 9: Scouting the Competition to Learn the Best Monetization Practices 89

Chapter 10: Advertising 92

Chapter 11: Affiliate marketing 101

Chapter 12: Facebook Marketing 118

Who's On Facebook? 119

How Might You Market on Facebook? 120

The Most Effective Method to Market with Pages 122

Profile Photo and Cover Image 123

Post Useful Information to Your Timeline 125

Ask Your Fans Questions 126

Varieties of Facebook Ads 128

Chapter 13: Monitor Your Analytics 134

What Are Analytics? 135

Pay Attention to Popular Titles and Articles 136

Collect Data to See What Exactly People Like 137

Be Sure to Consider What People Don't Like, Too .. 138

Post More Content That Will Earn Likes and Shares 140

Never Stop Checking Your Analytics 141

Chapter 14: Income Streams 143

Chapter 15: Start Selling from Day One 153

Chapter 16: Branding your Blog and other Online Platforms 157

Chapter 17: Email Marketing 167

Chapter 18: The Pros and Cons of Blogging 173

Chapter 19: Avoiding Common Mistakes 179

Chapter 20: How to Keep Your Traffic Coming Back?.184

   Repurpose Old Content 184

   Engage with Your Audience 187

Chapter 21: Maintaining a Blog for Your Business 191

   1. Write for the customers 192

   2. Plan the content beforehand.................................193

   3. Write the content in a constructive manner..........194

   4. See that posts are short and sweet 195

   5. How often should you update your blog?.............195

   6. See that responsibility is shared among team members 196

   7. Draw your inspiration from customers.................197

   8. Use the necessary imagery 198

   9. Respond to queries and complaints......................199

Conclusion..200

Introduction

Starting a blog and making it successful requires hard work and dedication. It is only logical to seek ways to monetize it and be rewarded for all that hard work. The challenge for most bloggers is finding a monetization method that works.

Even if you're blogging just because you love writing or you just enjoy creating online content, you should still consider monetizing your blog. This way, your hobby will be able to support you financially. A financially successful blog will allow you to survive while doing what you love.

In this book, we will discuss the different ways of how you can make money with your blog. The best method differs for each blog. We will discuss each one so that you can decide which will be best for your website and for the type of content you offer.

The book discusses successful methods of monetizing your blog by focusing on methods that have been tested and proven. They are still used by the most successful blogs today.

When it comes to blog monetization, there is no reason to start from scratch. Your website will earn faster if you use these reliable ways of making money. While it will require some trial and error, in the beginning, the tips in this book will help bridge the information gap and increase the rate of success for your blog.

The chapters of this book include details on how to start publishing advertisements on your blog, how to start an affiliate marketing business, and how to sell your own products and services. The book also contains less popular yet effective ways of making money.

Most importantly, this book guides you on how you can connect with your audience and actually increase the effectiveness of your monetization process. It discusses how you learn where your audience comes from and how you can gain their trust to improve sales and click-through rates.

I hope you enjoy it. Thanks!

Chapter 1

How to Start a Blog?

Blogging is much more than simply just writing. There is a lot that goes into the making of a successful blog. Blog design, platform, and sharing are some important factors you need to keep in mind while creating your blog. Now that you've decided to run a blog let us help you with a definitive guide on how to create a blog. The following steps are absolutely prudent for anyone who wants to start a blog:

Step 1: Choose the topic you want to blog about

Are you going to run a blog on feminism, or will you focus on recipes? Is it a DIY fashion blog that you want to be known for? In any case, before you start putting your articles and your blog posts out there on the internet for everyone to see, it is important that you have a clear idea of what you are going to blog about.

Your writing should be different and inspiring, so it needs to be about something that you are passionate about. Unless you are passionate about what you're writing and know a fair deal about it, you will find it difficult to keep the blog going. So, first things first- know the central theme of your blog. It'll help you envision your blog structure much better.

Step 2: Pick your blogging platform

This is where you actually get started. Now is the part where you choose where you want to build your blog. I would suggest that you go for Word Press as it is one of the biggest and popular platforms for blogging. Word Press allows for multiple plugins, offers a variety of themes and layout choices. Word Press is really easy to set-up, which is why we suggest that you pick Word Press as your platform. Word Press currently has about 82 million users. We don't need to tell you that it's a huge number now. Do we?

However, there are a few more alternatives that you may pick. These include, but are not restricted to:

Blogger

This is one of the earliest blogging platforms and is really easy to set up as well. It is best suited for lifestyle bloggers or first-time bloggers, but it is not the ideal choice for full-fledged websites or business-related blogs.

Tumbler

This is a microblogging site that works like a mix between a social networking site and a blogging platform. It allows for a lot of interaction and is really simple to use. With Yahoo having bought it recently, ads might be in the near future, but other than that, there aren't a lot of cons. This is the best option if you are catering to the youth and are not looking to run a very serious blog. However, it is not ideal for long articles or long-term blogging.

Medium

Medium is fairly new, only having been started recently in 2012. This site has a great layout, allows for good interaction, and is regarded as one of the top blogging platforms at the moment. There is a lack of customization, but that apart from that, the platform is minimalistic and efficient.

All options considered, I still urge you to opt for Word Press as it is efficient, easy to start, and uncomplicated to run.

Step 3: Free alternative or self-hosting? Time to make the cut!

This is an important step in creating a blog. You need to decide whether you are going to pay for the website or whether you will use a free one. There are advantages and disadvantages of both the options, so you need to weigh them carefully and then make your decision.

While a free blog sounds great for those of us who are not interested in very serious blogging, there are many limitations to it. You will neither be able to avail all services offered by blogging platforms such as Blogger, Word Press, etc., such as their themes nor will you ever own a domain name. There is a restriction to the amount of content that you can put up, which is not the case when you own your blog. Since you are using a free platform, the content you put up might be deleted anytime, since it is not on your own web property. Can you imagine losing all your hard work in a flash? Yikes!

If you don't intend to take up blogging as a serious activity and don't think that you'll be posting very frequently, we suggest you refrain from a self-hosting blog. It's not like a self-hosting blog is ever a bad idea, but if you're a casual blogger, then it's not very prudent that you buy your space.

Step 4: Domain and Hosting

The domain is essentially nothing but your blog URL, so pick your blog domain after careful consideration. It should be catchy and unique. Since it is the first point of contact between you and your target audience, make sure you pick something that'll attract them. Also, it is a good idea to include a keyword in your domain name. For example, if you're going to blog about food, make sure that something culinary related and common is a part of your domain name.

Once you have selected a domain name, it is time to register it on a host website. Confused? Don't be. You require a company to put your website up on the internet for everybody to see. Most hosting companies have a hassle-free, one-click Word Press installation on their admin panels. There is a wide array to pick from, so select one that is best suited to your functionality and is economical. Having picked your hosting website, you should now install your choice of blogging platform on it.

Step 5: Blog Layout and Design

This is the most fun part of creating a blog-you get to decide how it looks! There are generally a lot of themes that you can pick from, some of them free and some of them paid. Pick according to your convenience, sift through them, and settle on a theme that you think is the most compatible with the kind of content you will put up. It should be clean, not confusing, and easy to navigate for the audience. The correct layout is absolutely essential, because your blog is a reflection of your personality, and you do not want to undermine great content with a layout that is dastardly and unappealing. Make your readers focus their attention on your blog, provide them with an enriching experience that'll keep them engaged, and motivate them to read more of your work in the future. The right layout helps in doing so.

Web plugins, links to social media, etc. are additions that you may make later on, but the five steps mentioned above are the essentials of starting a blog. Basic knowledge as aforementioned is sufficient for you to start a blog of your own and get posting.

Chapter 2

NICHE

When you create a blog, you need a niche, and if you don't already have one, then you should start thinking about one.

There are entire books written about choosing a good niche, and while there is a certain science to finding a profitable niche, I strongly tend to disagree with the notion that earning money with a blog is all about finding a profitable niche. Anyone who is telling you this is filling your head with utter nonsense. As you'll soon learn, the niche you choose is largely irrelevant.

What I teach is that you write your own blog, and you write it from your heart. You should be open, honest, as transparent as possible, and you provide your audience with a highly sincere level of value that they can't get anywhere else. This is the true key to maintaining a following and to earning a profit with your blog.

The reality is that the best niche for you to write about will always be the niche that you are most passionate about, something you love. If you truly love what you are writing about, then there is a very high chance that a bunch of other people out there will love it too!

Frankly speaking, you have a higher chance of being successful blogging about some niche that never seemed like it could be profitable if you are passionate about that niche than if you try to pick some niche just based on the fact that you are targeting profitable keywords. The big money bloggers only blog about what they are highly passionate about, and so this is the path I recommend to you as well.

Look at it this way. If your true passion happens to be little yellow pebbles, then blog about little yellow pebbles. The more unique your niche is, the less competition you'll have, and if you're the only one with a solid blog on the topic, then you'll have no competition at all. Though that doesn't mean that you should avoid blogging in niches that may seem oversaturated, as the reason that many niches seem to be oversaturated is because there is a very large audience in those niches who can't get enough of the information they crave, so there is plenty of room for many more bloggers to jump in and capitalize on that traffic. Though the reality is that only the bloggers who are the most passionate about what they are blogging about will be able to acquire a long-term dedicated following, which is the goal that you should be striving for with your blog.

There are bloggers out there making a full-time salary writing in the most insane niches that you may have never even realized a profit could be earned from, so if you're truly passionate about little yellow pebbles and really want to write about them, then my answer to you would be: Well, you seem very passionate about it, so you definitely have a winning niche there!

Niche truly does fail to be an issue if you have something that you are totally heads over heels, ultra-passionate about. And if you don't have that, then you need to think a lot harder in order to figure out exactly what you are really passionate about, because the reality of the situation is that if you don't have something that you're totally passionate about, then you don't really have a blog worth writing.

Any blog you create about something that you are not passionate about is not going to get you very far in the blogging world and is doomed to fail, unless your only aim is targeting cheap traffic for short-term profit, but such a blog won't be sustainable in the long-term, so why waste your time with something unsustainable.

I mean, let's face the facts. If you create a blog, you're going to have to write blog posts regularly, and writing is already hard work as it is, and writing about something you just kind of feel so-so about is going to seem more like more of a chore compared to something that you are totally excited to write about.

Thus, you really have to take a liking to what you are blogging about. Think about what a miserable existence you would have if you regularly blogged about a topic that you truly have no interest in whatsoever. Would you enjoy that? How long could you do it for? Week? Months? Years? The chances are that such a pursuit would cause you to eventually quit blogging altogether and never come back to it.

And so, I hope this chapter clarifies the whole question of the niche in that you need to blog in the area that you are the most passionate about. If you're not passionate about anything, then your job should be to put your blog on hold, put down this book, and find your passion first. Once you've found your passion, you're then ready to start your blog.

Because let's face it. You're going to be writing about your niche a lot, and so it must be something you actually like, and even better is if it is something that you truly love! No matter what any niche analysis expert tells you, this is the truth of the matter.

Let's take a look at the stock market, which is nothing more than a list of companies in different niches. Does anyone know which stocks will go up or down or which company will be successful or fail? Despite all of the expert analysis and empirical data on the matter, not one of the experts can claim to really know.

It cannot be denied that the companies that are most successful in the long-term are those companies where the people who run them are truly passionate about the product or service that their company provides, and blogging is no different since the bottom line of blogging is that your blog is a company.

You heard me right the first time; your blog is a company! If you think otherwise, it would be a mistake. Even if it's not turning a profit yet, the moment you earn your first commission, you're suddenly a company. Even if you try to argue that you're not a company, if your blog is monetized and earning a profit, then I can guarantee that the tax authorities won't believe your "my blog is not a company" story.

And so, in the fashion of all great companies, you want to start off on the right foot by starting something great from the get-go with your blog, and this means that having passion for what you're going to be blogging about is the single most important defining element of success for you.

What is the reason most blogs fail? It's that the people who started them were not passionate enough about their blogs and decided to give up and do something else. Don't let that be you!

Let's not fool ourselves; passion is everything in this business! So no matter what your niche may be, it should be that thing that you feel most passionate about, and if it isn't, then you're setting yourself up for failure as well as a completely empty existence.

I could keep telling you why it's important that you blog about something that you are extremely passionate about, so rather than go on and on about it, I leave you with this final thought: If you read some random person's blog about a niche you happen to like, will you continue to read it if it was written with a ton of passion behind it (even if the writing itself is not so spectacular)? How about a similar blog in the same niche written by someone with an equal level of writing skill who just didn't seem so passionate about it at all? I think you know the answer, and based on that, I rest my case.

Thus, I hope you are one of the lucky ones who knows what you are passionate about and doesn't have to put this book down to think about it. Because without having a passion, there really isn't any point in moving forward. So if you don't have a passion, then please do us all a favor and put this book down and start thinking about it, and come back when you have one.

What should your niche be? It should most definitely be what you are most passionate about!

Choose Your Design

Now that you know what you want to talk about and who you want to be talking to, you need to begin thinking about what you want your blog to look like. Believe it or not, the design of your blog plays a big role in how people will perceive you. Experts say that if a person lands on your website and is not clear on what to do or attracted to it within the first 10 seconds, they will just as quickly click back off of your website. This means that you have to capture their attention and drive their focus in about 10 seconds. Your design is exactly what will help you with that.

When it comes to a blog, you do not need to invest in a fancy or expensive web designer to get it to where you want to be. At least, not right away. If that is something you choose to invest in later in the future, that is a great idea. This can help maximize the flow of your website, increase the aesthetics, and take you from small-time professional to the big leagues. Still, it is not necessary early on. In fact, it is not even recommended early on. While you do want an appealing and easy-to-navigate website, you do not want to go into debt before you start earning income. Wait until your blog begins generating a steady income before you begin investing in expensive designers and graphics. In the meantime, take advantage of these four tips to help you.

Think About What You Like

You have already been browsing other blogs to get an idea of what topic is going to help you generate success. So, that means you have already been navigating other blogs that are similar to the one that you want to create. By now, you should have a clear understanding with regard to what you like and what you don't like on a blog. You may have encountered various features or graphics that drew you in and others that you were not attracted to at all. Consider these reactions. These will help you determine how you want your own blog to look.

Although your blog appearance is meant to draw others in, remember that you should enjoy it, too. If you do not enjoy the blog that you are creating, you simply won't feel the drive to continue working toward it. Getting to that point will take a significant amount of time and energy, and it won't feel good creating financial freedom for yourself. You should enjoy this process as much as your audience will.

Choose One That Will Reflect Your Topic

Another thing that you need to consider that many people don't is how your design reflects your topic. Believe it or not, different aesthetics are used depending on what you are talking about. If you are talking about a topic that involves a lot of pictures, such as photography, you will want a design that highlights the photographs you are taking while also providing ample space for you to share your verbal opinion. If your topic revolves more about opinion and topics, however, and not graphics, you may want one that highlights your conversation more.

Additionally, the entire format of your page varies depending on who you are targeting. Some blogs will revolve solely around blog entries whereas others feature other pages, too. These sometimes include "evergreen content," such as your most popular blog posts or ones that tend to be read more than once, resources, product information, and guides, or even various categories of your blog itself. Pay attention to what you want your design to feature so that you can choose one that is going to allow you to accurately reflect the topic that you are talking about.

Pick One That Is Aesthetically Appealing

Remember, the first ten seconds are all you have to draw someone in. You need to pick a blog that is going to be aesthetically appealing, and that will draw people in right away. They should feel immediately drawn in to look further. Consider your design as your packaging. This is the "packaging" that your blog is packed in, and if it is not appealing, people likely won't care about what is inside. Instead, they will be drawn to look elsewhere.

It may sound shallow, but aesthetics amount to a lot when it comes to blogging. You need a design that has easy to read colors, graphics that are attractive and focused, and a clear "purpose." People should land on your blog and know exactly what topic you will be discussing in all of your content. There should be no guessing or confusion. They should also immediately be drawn to the key areas of your blog such as your blog itself or your products or services associated with your blog.

Finally, you need an aesthetic and design that works. There is nothing worse than landing on a blog where the design does not flow well, pages are not properly designed, and ultimately, you are uncertain about how anything works. Broken hyperlinks, incomplete pages, an enormous number of visible grammatical and spelling errors, and other such factors can quickly drive people to search for the same content elsewhere. Your page design should function properly if you are going to get anything from it. Think about professionalism in every way that you can, especially with your design.

Consider What Your Audience Would Like

Remember, your blog is not just about you. You need to consider what your audience is going to be most drawn to, too. This is a chance for you to go back to those ten blogs you originally researched and look them over once more. What do the most popular blogs have in common? What do the least popular blogs in common? Can you say anything apart based on how they are designed? Often, the more popular blogs will have common features and so, too, will the least popular ones. Pay attention to these themes and trends, as you will want to implement the ones being used by popular blogs. This is how you can make your blog look "flashy" and professional right from the start. Learn from the mistakes of other bloggers with regard to their design so that when it comes to your own blog, you can skip past the mistakes and errors and move straight toward success!

Chapter 3

Domains and hosting

When Starting out with your blog, it can be tempting to use a free site. After all, you're still posting a blog that's available on the internet, so why pay more than you really have to, to set up? Free blog services are fine if you're not really taking this seriously and just doing it as a hobby, but if you're trying to make this your full-time income/ business doing this will have major disadvantages that will only make life harder.

Free sites usually won't rank as well in search engines like paid domain names. They also don't give you control over your design, making the page look less unique and professional. Some of the free services out there also run their own ads on your website, which limits your chances of making ad income.

Domain names

A domain name is simply that part of the address of your website that is between "www." and ".com." You can find a unique domain name through various online services. A domain that has been registered may not be off limits; some people will buy domains to re-sell them though these are often far more expensive options.

You can register your domain name for a limited amount. For example, you can register a new domain name with GoDaddy for only $10 a year. There are services apart from this that offer domain registration from $20 to $40. Domain names vary a lot in prices, depending on their demand and attractiveness.

For a while when the first internet business boom was happening, investors would buy domain names for reselling them at a higher price, with some going for thousands or even millions of dollars (sex.com sold for $13 million in 2010, the current record; investing.com sold for $2.5 million in 2012). The bubble on this industry has burst, however, and even the most in-demand domains have seen their prices fall back down to earth.

You should try to buy a domain name that closely matches the name you have chosen for your blog. It is not a necessity though. You are free to put whatever content you want to on your website. However, if you have the same domain name and blog name, it will help you in creating recognition for your brand. It will also help your readers when they try to search you on the internet.

First, you need to brainstorm some words and phrases that pertain to your selected niche. Then, think of some related ideas. Once you've decided on a combination that you are satisfied with, you can search whether that combination is available through an online registration service. Usually, titles comprising one word (particularly those in popular subjects) are already purchased by a domain investor who wants to sell them at a profit. This means you will find them a bit expensive.

Let's use the example of the vegan comfort food cooking blog. Cooking and vegan are common words that are likely to be already used or, at least, to have been purchased by an investor. Think about the next level of your niche, then—the comfort food angle—and brainstorm possible combinations.

Word combinations that comprise of two or more words are more likely to be available. With some brainstorming, you can get a domain name that is pertinent to your niche and is available for use. Try to make it unique as well so that people can easily remember it.

Hosting

After you decide a domain name, you have got an address for it, but your blog doesn't have a home at this point. You also need a server to host all files related to your site so that your viewers can access them. There are different hosting sites that provide such services. If you select a company that offers both domain registration and hosting services, it would be convenient. However, you should make sure that the site fulfills all your requirements before you sign up for it. Blue Host is one such hosting site for WordPress bloggers who are transitioning to a self-sufficient site.

The most important thing to consider is how much web traffic volume you can have on a particular hosting site. Bandwidth limits won't matter when you're first starting your blog, but if you hope to grow your traffic quickly, you shouldn't set yourself up for failure by choosing a server that's too small. A lot of hosting sites offer different tiers of packages at different rates depending on your traffic needs and make it easy to upgrade down the line.

You can typically pay for hosting month by month, and while you usually get a bit of a discount for buying more time at once, paying monthly can let you try a service out if you're not sure whether or not it will work for you. Moving hosts can be a hassle but isn't as costly or difficult as changing domains would be; you can change your mind in the future without affecting your readers' ability to access your pages.

When you start your blog, you can choose a shared hosting account, which is usually the cheapest option available. You can get these services for about $1-$2 per month. Some of the sites that offer the option of shared hosting account are iPage, eHost, and In Motion Hosting. You must do thorough research before you sign up. Special focus should be on the reliability and quality of customer service. You can also check their feedback from other bloggers.

Site builders and CMS

You've got a domain name and a host where the files associated with it can live. Now, you need to make your blog and transfer it to the host—and if you're not a technically-minded person, this can be very intimidating.

The level of involvement you want to have with the creation of the page code on your site will determine which kind of site editor or site builder is best for you. People use these terms in different ways, adding to the confusion.

A web editor gives you the most control over your page's design, but it also requires some knowledge of HTML and CSS, and probably also things like JavaScript, PHP, and Perl for the kind of components most people want on a blog. The most basic web editor is a plain text program like Notepad. Plain text programs will require you to write all the code but are the cheapest and most straightforward option.

Web editor programs like Dreamweaver and KompoZer have a visual interface for the user, making the website-building experience more similar to designing a Word document than to writing computer code.

Once you've designed your pages with a web editor, you still need to get them onto your host's server using an FTP (File Transfer Protocol) program. Both the FTP program and the web editor will need to be installed on your computer, and you have complete control over their use, which is the primary advantage of using this method.

An online site builder is similar to a website editor except run entirely online instead of through your computer. Site builder services are provided by larger web hosting companies (such as GoDaddy) though often for an extra fee. The online site designer will have a similar interface as a web editor like Dreamweaver or KompoZer. Since you're building your sites directly on the host though, you don't have to worry about uploading them with an FTP program, and you can use any device to edit your website, not only one computer with the software installed.

Even if you're using site editing software or an online site builder, basic knowledge of at least HTML and CSS will be very helpful in making your site look and feel the way you want. Even if you don't know how to code them, you should understand what they do and be able to interpret them when you see them.

You will also need a Content Management System (CMS). It is software that you need to install on your web host. This will help in streamlining the addition of important features like tags and categories for pages, search and archive functions, or forums and comment sections.

When you use site builders or site editors, each of these features will have to be added manually, which can be incredibly time-consuming even if you are a web-coding expert. Content management systems also make it a lot easier to redesign the look of your overall site.

CMS software does take up space on your server and websites run with a CMS use more RAM and CPU than those made using a site editor. On high traffic days, this could mean your pages are slow to load or could cause problems with resource limits if you're using a shared server.

You also don't get quite as much creative control over the features and design elements of the page as you would by designing it completely on your own. The key benefit of CMS software is that you can focus on content generation instead of worrying about issues such as fixing lines of code or manually adjusting your pages when you change to a new layout. This will allow you to focus on your core strengths.

There are many CMS programs available on the internet; some of them are also specific for bloggers. The good part is that many are free as well. WordPress is probably the most well-known among them. Although WordPress is a free blogging site, it can also be downloaded as software and installed on your domain.

However, it's not necessary to opt for WordPress. You can research the features you would need and like to have for your site. Just like with changing domain names, changing CMS software can be a headache and a half if you have to do it down the road.

Chapter 4

TYPES OF BLOGS

You might have come across different types of blogs on the Internet, which may fall under many different types. Depending on the purpose of your blog, what you are already writing or what you are thinking about writing, you can find any of the following types by looking around on the Internet:

1. Niche blogs

These are the kind of blogs consisting of information relating to a particular niche that has the potential to bring in money. Niche bloggers write content related to popular topics like celebrities, beauty and makeup, movies, gadgets, or credit cards that appeal to the general public. Such bloggers aim to make money by posting ads and affiliate links on their blogs. Most of the ads are usually of the "pay-per-click" type, which is content-specific. For example, on a makeup and beauty blog, you will most likely find ads related to products generally used by women. Another way bloggers will make money with a niche blog is by doing product reviews and giving their honest feedback on products that are related to the niche they are writing about. Again, a beauty blog may review a new mascara product that is on the market in return for free product and usually a small fee. In other cases, the aim of the blog is to redirect readers to another website, which in turn tries to sell them a product. Niche bloggers are usually driven by a motivation to make money from their blogs, which are usually vast in numbers.

2. Business blogs

These blogs are maintained by business owners to support their businesses. Whatever the business might be, such blogs provide quality content to users about a topic related to the business. The business owner doesn't see the blog as a source of income but sees it as a marketing tool to promote his or her business. An example of a business blog could be a deck and fencing company. They would have a blog that could discuss the types of materials you can use to build a deck or fence as well as many of the designs that they use in their construction projects. The blog wouldn't make any money, but it would send people who are searching for similar topics to his site, thereby increasing business.

3. Professional blogs

A professional blog consists of the elements that make up both niche blogs and business blogs. Owners of professional blogs see their blogs as a part of their business. Blogs that offer services like e-courses, consulting services, or sell digital products online come under this category. Such businesses usually do not have an offline presence. This means their whole business is run online and does not have a store or an office in the real world. Such bloggers usually provide users with quality content, as it is the keystone of their business. An example of a blog that would fall under this category is a business that is selling homemade crocheted products. There may be blog posts to discuss different yarns and hooks, as well as free patterns available. Then there would also be patterns that need to be purchased as well as the links to purchase goods from the owner of the business.

4. Personal blogs

Personal blogs have a narrative tone and cover the personal experiences of the blogger. These blogs are personal journals and are more of a hobby to their owners and are not monetized like niche or professional blogs. Such bloggers just want to have fun online by sharing their experiences in a casual, witty tone. Their main goal is not to attract customers but to make new friends online. Some of these blogs are regularly updated while others don't see an update for months. The most common theme among these blogs is parenting blogs. As every parent has different experiences, no two blogs are the same, and many parents visit these blogs as a way to get new ideas when it comes to raising their children. This also allows parents to connect to one another as well as support one another.

5. Media-type blogs

The type of media used to express the author's thoughts online defines these blogs. For instance, a blog that consists of photographs is called a photoblog. A vlogger is a blogger who uses videos to share thoughts. An art blog consists of sketches and other artwork by the blog owner. Blogs that express content in the form of comics are called comic blogs. These blogs can fall into the same category of personal blogs. These blogs can also be used to make money or to support a cause.

6. Reverse blogs

For reverse blogs, the owner is not the same as the content provider. Public users usually provide the content in the form of guest posts. A moderator, so as to prevent the publishing of unpleasant or offending content, monitors such posts. These blogs normally attract a large number of followers as there are more opinions and more content for readers to see. Since there are usually multiple posters to the blog, it is often updated more frequently which engages readers more than those being updated less often.

Here, we will point out some major reasons why you should start a blog. Everyone has their own reasons for starting to blog, and chances are if you are reading this book, at least one of the following reasons is going to apply to you. Hopefully, by the time you are done reading, you will be raring to begin a blog of your own.

Chapter 5

GETTING STARTED WITH WRITING A NEW BLOG

Every new blogger wants to know what it takes to write a good blog. Here are the steps you need to follow to if you are new to blogging and hoping someone would tell you how to get started with writing a blog:

Plan your blog post

Contrary to popular belief, writing a blog post will not just take a couple of hours. Several days might pass between the day you have started writing the blog and the day you submit it for publication. Irrespective of your vocabulary, writing style, or typing speed, it may take anywhere up to a week to finish and review your blog. You can decrease this time by properly planning your blog beforehand. Before you sit down to write, you need to see you have everything you need to write the blog. You can save a lot of time doing your homework beforehand. Many new bloggers are unaware or skip the planning process, but if you want to submit your blog on time, take a look at the steps involved in planning a blog:

Try to choose a topic in which you are interested

It is not that you shouldn't write on a topic that doesn't interest you, but if you don't enjoy what you write, the reader can't enjoy it either. If you choose to write on a topic that doesn't interest you, your lack of enthusiasm will show in your writing, which is more than enough to kill a blog post. If you are bored with the topic, how can you expect the reader to find the blog engaging?

But not everyone has the freedom to choose the topic of his or her blog post. Freelancers are usually hired by blog owners to write on a topic that is essential for the blog owner's business. It is not always that they are asked to write on interesting topics. Writing some blogs may feel like a chore, especially if the topic is boring or doesn't interest them. For instance, a freelancer might be asked to write about cardboards by a company that manufactures cardboard boxes. Cardboard boxes hardly make up an interesting topic to write about, but what choice does the freelancer have if he takes on the project? In such cases, it is the responsibility 0f the writer to accept the blandness of the topic and turn it into something interesting with his or her writing style. After all, that is their vocation. But when you do have a choice to pick a topic for your blog, go for the one that interests you. That way, you will enjoy what you write and don't have to put in much effort to make the blog engaging and interesting for the readers. Your enthusiasm will definitely show in your writing, and that is what makes a blog good.

Make an outline of what you want to write

It is essential that you make an outline of what you are thinking when writing on a blog post. The outline doesn't have to be detailed or long; it should just be able to give you an idea of what you are planning to write and in what order you are planning to present information. This outline will guide you after you begin writing the actual blog and will prevent you from deviating from the topic and start rambling unknowingly.

For example, let us suppose you are writing a blog about the adventure sport of mountaineering. The outline for the blog would look something like this:

- **Introduction**

  - Few lines explaining what the blog is about

- **Section 1 – Prerequisites for mountaineering**

  - The physical and mental requirements that a mountaineering enthusiast needs to meet to take up the sport

- **Section 2 – Mountaineering institutes**

  - List of mountaineering institutes that train people for the sport

- **Section 3 – Popular mountaineering destinations**

  - List of popular mountaineering destinations and their difficulty levels

- **Section 4 – Things to carry**

  - List of mountaineering equipment and other essential things that need to be carried by mountaineers

- **Section 5 – Tips to deal with altitude sickness**

    - Explaining the symptoms of altitude sickness and suggesting foods, exercises, and medicines that help in controlling the sickness

- **Section 6 – Do's and don'ts of mountaineering**

- **Section 7 – Conclusion- wrapping up the blog post with an inspiring quote.**

The outline prepared thus far gives you a rough idea on what to cover and the order in which the information needs to be presented to your readers. Preparing such outlines beforehand saves you a lot of time, as it dictates in what direction you need to think and for what information you need to perform your research. It will also prevent you from deviating from the topic. For example, you might feel tempted to bring up the movie in which a man amputates his own hand in order to survive a mountaineering accident. It's not exactly off topic, but it definitely deviates from the tone of the blog post. You are not exactly writing about "the survival techniques to follow when your arm gets stuck under a boulder," so it is important you do not deviate from post's topic. And writing an outline is one way to ensure against such deviation.

Get your facts right

Not all professional bloggers know everything before sitting down to write about a topic. The same goes for you. You don't have to have knowledge about a topic to write down a blog about it. Not everyone can know everything, and when it comes to bloggers, it is not their knowledge but their natural curiosity that allows them to switch between blogs relating to different topics. They dig deep to study and research about a topic before sitting down to write about it. You can follow suit whenever you are required to write about a topic in which you have no knowledge. But, there is one mistake that most bloggers make while researching a topic. And that's getting your facts from Wikipedia as your sole source of information.

Wikipedia does have a collection of articles that have been researched before getting published, but factual errors creep up in the text sometimes, as the articles are not contributed by a single person but by anyone who wishes to make a contribution. There may be several people behind the publication of an article in Wikipedia. Errors may creep up as the community collects information from various sources. So, as a responsible blogger, you need to check your facts before presenting them in a blog. Instead of collecting information from Wikipedia alone, refer to official websites of products, government websites, researched articles, and articles by industry experts. It is human nature to make mistakes. So, it is necessary you approach information with skepticism and keep questioning and researching things until you are positive that the information you have collected is top notch and does not have any factual errors.

Focus on the headlines

A blog headline is what will primarily show in the search results and is responsible for grabbing eyeballs.

The working title

A working title is a very specific sentence or phrase and tells exactly what the blog is about. For example, the working title for the topic "weight loss" can be any one of the following:

- ❖ How drinking more water helps you lose weight
- ❖ Five fat-free recipes that should be a part of your weight-loss journey
- ❖ Top five exercises you need to add to your workout regimen to burn fat quickly

Notice that the three titles are very specific but are not particularly catchy. But, before you start pulling in your creativity to think of a perfect title for your blog, you can start writing the blog with the working title as the headline. You can worry about making it eye catchy and clickable either after you finish writing the blog or during the writing stage.

See that the headline is accurate.

Accuracy is the key when it comes to deciding on a headline for your blog. When you zero in on a title that is accurate, you are setting clear expectations for the audience. Let us suppose the working title of your blog is "How drinking more water helps you lose weight."

The title can be modified to "How drinking water helps you lose more weight way easily as compared to weight-loss diets or products available in the market..." which might attract attention, as it claims water is better than weight-loss diets or weight-loss products when it comes to helping a person in losing weight. But, has the blogger provided proof for the claim in the body section of the blog? Or is the title a mere exaggeration of the actual facts?

When you raise the expectation of the reader through the headline, and when you fail to deliver in the body section, readers get disappointed, which may result in the loss of readership. Nothing angers a reader more than a misleading headline.

Use numbers

The reason why the majority of blogs use numbers in their headlines is simple. People like numbers, so they grab people's attention. You can see it for yourself with a simple experiment. Just type the words "weight-loss diet" in Google search and in the top search results you can find headlines like "7-day weight- loss diet plan,"

"20 most weight loss friendly foods" or "Top 50 foods for weight loss." Or simply, you can pick any magazine that's near you and scan through the headlines of the front-page articles. You will see almost every headline uses a numeral. There aren't any specific rules when it comes to number usage in a headline, but if you want to really catch people's attention, using rarely-used numerals, like 17 or 37, can help your title.

Use effective language

Playing with words can certainly make your title pop when it comes to grabbing people's attention. Here are the ways you can make your headline stand out from among a list of search results:

Play with alliteration:

Usage of alliterations imparts interestingness and subtlety to a headline. Think of the movie title 'Fantastic Four' or even the title of this book "Blogging Guide." Don't you think such alliterations are not only eye-catchy but also easy to remember?

Don't be afraid to use strong language:

Plain language does a bad job of grabbing attention. Don't be afraid to use strong language like, "Things People Hate," "Ground-Breaking," or "Kick-Ass." For example, consider the following two titles that have been chosen for the same blog:

"Reasons Why People Don't Like Mondays"

"5 Things People Hate About Mondays"

Which title do you think is the most eye-catching between the two? It has to be the second one, as it is not only accurate but also precisely describes how people feel on Mondays using the word "hate." But, see that you don't overdo it as too much of boldness might affect the subtlety of the title.

Play with adjectives:

Adjectives add strength to an expression, so you can make use of them to make your headlines more impactful. Here are the examples of adjectives that could make your headline more interesting:

- ❖ Painstaking
- ❖ Free
- ❖ Strange
- ❖ Hilarious
- ❖ Best/Worst
- ❖ Brilliant
- ❖ Fool-proof
- ❖ Stunning
- ❖ Incredible
- ❖ Absolute
- ❖ Shocking
- ❖ Essential
- ❖ Effortless
- ❖ Fun
- ❖ Easy

Words to be used with list posts:

Certain words will add to the interestingness of list posts. Here are a few examples:

❖ Lessons:
Example: 5 Life Lessons We Can Learn from the Movie Ratatouille

❖ Tips:
Example: Tips to Improve Your Vocabulary

❖ Ways:
Example: 5 Effective Ways to Lose Weight Fast

❖ Tricks:
Example: Top 25 Windows Tricks and Tips

❖ Facts:
Example: 10 Facts You Didn't Know About Hitler

❖ Ideas:
Example: Top 20 Low-Cost Business Ideas for Beginners

❖ Secrets:
Example: 8 Hollywood Beauty Secrets You Need to Know

❖ Reasons:
Example: Top 10 Reasons Why You Shouldn't Get Married

Use trigger words:

When you can't use a number in your headline, an alternative way to make sure your headline grabs attention is to use trigger words like "Why, What, When, Where or How." These words help a great deal in persuading someone to read a blog post:

Examples:

    a) Reasons Why You Should Drink More Water
    b) Situations Where You need to be Assertive
    c) How to Write an Effective Essay

Run a quick search

If you are considering using a title such as "Top Ten Reasons You Should Drink More Water," quickly run it through a search engine such as Google. By doing this, you are going to see how many other blog writers have used the same title in their blogs. There isn't anything wrong with using the same title when it is generic such as in the example above. However, it is important to realize that when your blog is coming up in the search engine, there are going to be many other blogs also coming up in the search results.

Keep the title short.

However big the blog post may be that you are writing, it is always advised you keep the title short, preferably fewer than or equal to 65 characters. It was found that blogs and websites with shorter titles rank well in search engine results. Also, if you are keen to share the link of your blog on social networking sights like Twitter, see that the title doesn't exceed 117 characters. The character limit in Twitter is 140, so the remaining 22 characters are for accommodating the URL. If you don't want the titles of your blogs to get cut off in the search engine results, try not to cross the threshold of 70 characters.

How to approach the body of the blog?

So far, you've been told how you should settle on a topic and how to think of a headline for a blog. Now, we will discuss how you need to approach the body of the blog.

There is no standard approach that needs to be followed when it comes to writing a blog. Bloggers, in general, follow one of the following approaches while writing a blog:

a) Finishing an entire blog post in a single sitting
b) Taking your time and chipping away at it over several short sittings

There is no right or wrong when it comes to following these approaches. You can choose the one that is the most suitable for your working style. However, it is advised you get most of your work done in a single sitting. By doing so, you can entirely focus on the topic, and get everything out of your head as soon as possible. If you think sitting several smaller sessions works for you, see that you utilize the time completely to fill in the content. If you keep on revisiting and revising the content you have written so far, you would be tempted to add information here and there, which could make your blog go off topic without you realizing it. Thus, even if you prefer to work on a single blog post over three to four shorter sessions, make sure you finish the majority of the writing in the first sitting itself. There's no need to worry if it takes a week or so to initially write a single blog. As you keep on writing blogs, the process becomes easier and more natural, thereby considerably reducing the time you need to spend writing a blog. As they say, practice makes perfect.

Make effective use of images.

People are visual in general and get attracted to images, especially the ones that illustrate the gist of the blog. It doesn't matter how well-written and how well-formatted the blog is. If suitable imagery is not used in the post, it won't take long before people lose interest and run screaming to Reddit or 9gag. Here are the points you need to remember about using imagery on your blog post:

1. When images are used at every juncture of the blog, it gives much-needed breaks between the paragraphs and makes the blog post look visually appealing.
2. Using the right imagery will impart humor to the post, which is a much-required characteristic these days to keep people engaged in your blog. Choosing the right image will serve as a visual punch line for the blog and help in generating a few laughs from the readers. Images come to your aid,

especially when the topic you are writing on is rather dry and boring. Thus, you should always employ images in your blog posts, especially if you want to make the post look interesting.
3. Using images will help make a topic easily understandable. Using infographics, charts, pie-diagrams, or tables assist in making the reader understand even the most complicated of topics. Thus, it is important that you employ appropriate imagery wherever required in the blog.

Editing the post

Editing what you have written is much harder than writing the blog itself. It is a common misconception among people that editing is all about correcting grammatical errors and striking the words or lines that don't fit into your post. It is true that sentence construction and grammar play an important role in determining the quality of the post; however, you need to remember that editing is not limited to fixing these things alone.

Editing also involves fixing the blog post in such a way that it doesn't have repetitive or unnecessary content. You should be able to see the post as a whole and willing to strike words or even paragraphs in order to maintain the coherence of the post. Apart from checking the spelling and grammar of your post, here are some tips and tricks you need to follow while editing the content:

Avoid the "crutch" words

See that you are not repeating the same words or phrases to describe many things. Writers tend to use their "crutch" word (a word they use very often in their writings) while talking about different things, so it is important that they are careful and not use the word too often. There is nothing more jarring for a reader than to read the same word again and again throughout a blog.

Read aloud what you've written.

This is one important trick they teach you writing workshops. After you finish writing your blog, start reading it aloud. If a sentence or a word sounds awkward when you're saying it loud, you need to modify or remove it. Also, if a phrase or a sentence seems to obstruct the flow of the post, remove it or keep rewriting it until it blends in with the rest of the post. You need to rework on the blog until the entire text slides off your tongue easily.

Ask someone else to read the post.

This is particularly important if you are new to blogging. You could ask a parent, friend, or colleague to read your post before you publish it. If they make a suggestion or two, consider them and see if their suggestions would improve the post. Some people might skip this step, as they feel that asking others to review their content is a sign of weakness. On the contrary, asking people close to you to review your post is a sign of commitment you have towards your blog.

Also, if you know someone who has editing experience, ask him or her to take a look at your work. Make sure to let them know that they don't have to look for spelling or grammatical errors, but that you need them to check the flow of the post and if it makes structural sense.

Accept the fact that the post will never be perfect.

Most novices become obsessed with the details and perfection of the post. They are usually very unforgiving of their work and keep on rewriting the same stuff in a bid to create the "perfect post." If you're one of them, you need to take it easy. It's important that your work is not sloppy, but it is also important for you to remember that there is nothing like a perfect blog. All you need to do is give your best, without obsessing over minor details and wasting time.

Chapter 6

Optimizing Your Blog For SEO

Tapping into The Gold Mine Of Traffic

When your blog is optimized for search engine traffic, you are tapping into the gold mine of traffic—Google. Google is the #1 site on the web that routinely gets millions of daily visitors who type various search terms to find the content they are looking for. Not all of these visitors will search for content related to your niche, but the number of people who search for content related to your niche may surprise you (hint: numerous people search for content related to your niche every day).

Some bloggers focus on SEO to such a high degree that search engine traffic accounts for most of their blog traffic. However, SEO appears as a next to impossible challenge for beginners. SEO is obviously doable since so many people get thousands of monthly visitors from

Google, but to the beginner, it looks like an impossible maze.

I remember when I first began my SEO journey and found myself in the nearly impossible maze. Which methods worked? Which methods were dead? Which methods would actually hurt instead of help you? Which methods were outdated? What are the new methods? Every question led right into the other, and mastering SEO couldn't have been more confusing. I read hundreds of blog posts and guidebooks that dealt with SEO, but I still had problems with SEO.

The lightbulb clicked when I decided to implement a few tactics at a time, master those tactics, and then move onto the next batch. Throughout this chapter, I will provide various tactics that are important for tapping into the gold mine of traffic. It is important for you to choose your favorite tactics, implement those first, master those tactics, and then move onto your next batch.

The SM-SEO Cycle

Social media and SEO complement each other very well. If your blog is properly optimized for each one, you will get more SEO and social media traffic in a continuous cycle. Search engines use social shares and social media activity to determine where your content ranks (among other things). As your blog posts accumulate more tweets, Facebook shares, pins, and other social shares, your blog will rank higher on search engines.

As your blog ranks higher on search engines because of social media activity and shares, your blog will get more search engine traffic. If your blog is properly optimized for social sharing, a higher percentage of your search engine visitors will share your blog posts on their social networks. That generates more activity on social media which leads to a higher rank on Google. That higher rank on Google leads to even more SEO traffic. This is the continuous SM-SEO cycle.

For my own blog, I have seen a direct correlation between my social media traffic and my SEO traffic.

Any day I got 300 visitors from social media, I got close to or a little more than 300 search engine visitors on those days. When I only got 200 visitors from social media in one day, I would get around 200 visitors from the search engines on that same day. Based on my experience, increasing your social media traffic also allows you to increase your SEO traffic.

Ever since I started my blog, my ratio of Twitter traffic to blog traffic in any given year (excluding 2012) has ranged from a 1 to 0.65 rate to a 1 to 1.15 ratio. The ratio is significant enough to determine that my SEO traffic relies largely in part on my social media traffic. For this particular case study, I only used Twitter since Twitter accounted for about 90% of my social media traffic.

Why Blog Speed Is Crucial For SEO And Your Blog's Success

Blog speed is increasingly gaining influence in how search engines rank our blogs. Faster blogs tend to rank higher than slower blogs because Google wants a quick transition between a click on one of the links that came up in the search result and the visitor seeing the content they expect to see.

Normally, a blog loads in a few seconds. Before our world got so fast, it would be acceptable for something to take a few seconds. Now, each extra second it takes for a blog to load is not as accepted. For every second it takes for a blog to load, page abandonment increases. If it takes more than four seconds to load, then 25% of your visitors will abandon your page before reading any of your content.

Blog speed also affects shopping behavior, and having a slow blog will decrease the likelihood of you getting customers. Here are some telling statistics from KISSmetrics that indicate how important blog speed is for customer behavior:

47% of consumers expect that the web page gets loaded in 2 seconds or even less.

79% of the dissatisfied shoppers are less likely to buy from the same site again.

52% of people shopping online say that quick page loading affects their site loyalty.

A one second delay (or three seconds of waiting) decreases customer satisfaction by about 16%.

44% of online shoppers are likely to share with their friends if they have a bad experience online.

A one second delay in page response can result in a 7% reduction in conversions.

These statistics make it clear that blog speed is not just important for search engines, but blog speed also determines what type of experience visitors have when they visit your blog. If your blog is fast, visitors will be more likely to stay loyal to your brand, but every extra second it takes for your website to load can have disastrous consequences. In the fast-paced world, we find that every second counts!

How To Make Your Blog Load Faster?

No matter how slow or fast your blog loads, making your blog load faster will allow you to attract visitors who stay on your blog for a longer period of time. There are several easy-to-do fixes that will allow your blog to load faster:

1. Have fewer blog posts on each page on your blog. When someone goes to your blog, it takes time to load each blog post. The more blog posts you have on one page of your blog, the longer it will take for your blog to load. I used to have 15 blog posts on each page, and it took a very long time for my blog to load. Ever since I decided to only show five blog posts per page, my blog has loaded faster since there is less content that needs to get loaded.

2. Remove extraneous pictures. When we first start our blogs, we tend to go out of control with the number of pictures we add to make our blogs look complete. When I created my blog, I stuffed my sidebar with pictures to make the sidebar more complete. Stuffing my sidebar with pictures made it take longer for my blog to load because loading all of those pictures takes time. It may take a few hundred milliseconds to load each picture, but those milliseconds add up to seconds, and that load

time doesn't include the other factors that slow down your blog. I used to have a big picture of myself on the sidebar to build brand recognition and a picture of my Twitter Domination Training course to get more sales. Taking down those two pictures made my blog load faster, and now instead of promoting the Twitter Domination Training course, I promote a free eBook which promotes the Twitter Domination Training course.

3. Make your own pictures. One of the most common mistakes bloggers make is getting pictures from other websites or Google images and putting those pictures in their blog posts. The problem with putting these pictures on your blog is that most of them take a lot of time to load. If it takes more than a second for one picture on your blog to load, then most of your visitors will abandon your blog before it loads. I made the same mistake as a rookie blogger, and that mistake hurt my blog's speed, and as a result, my search engine rank. The best pictures for blog speed are small pictures that you create on your own with a tool like Canva. All of the

pictures I create for my blog posts were created with Canva. They are 300 pixels by 300 pixels and don't take long to load. This one tactic made my blog load more than a second faster.
4. WordPress.org Users—Deactivate the plugins that you are not using. If your blog is powered by WordPress.org, then you have probably come across several plugins for your blog. Each activated plugin slows your blog down, and although some plugins have a big impact on your blog, other plugins do next to nothing for your blog. Deactivating the plugins you are not using will allow your blog to run faster.
5. Show a summary of your blog posts instead of the whole text. The text you put in your blog posts takes time to load, and if your blog posts consist of multiple pictures, then your blog loading time will get longer. You don't want to write shorter blog posts and not use pictures just because you are worried about your blog's loading time. The loophole to this issue is to show a summary of each of your blog posts on the homepage. Instead of showing the entire blog post, you can only show the first paragraph

by placing the More tag right after the first paragraph. Only showing one paragraph instead of your entire blog post and repeating that process for all of the blog posts on your homepage will make your blog load faster.

Chapter 7

Focus on Growing Your Audience

Something that you have to recognize in the blogging world is that, no matter how great your content is, you are not going to get any readers if you don't focus on growing your audience! Fortunately, growing your audience does not require you to invest significant amounts of money into advertisements and promotion. While this is certainly an option, and we will discuss it, the reality is that the best ways to promote your blog are actually free. You should only begin seeking to implement paid advertisements after you have a steady audience and are getting regular visitors to your page.

Look Beyond Your Website

Until now, a large portion of your focus has been solely on your website. You have focused on your topic, your design, and your content. Now, you need to begin looking outside of your website. You have done all that you can on your website to align yourself with your target audience and draw them in, but now you need to focus on creating "funnels" to draw them in through.

Funnels are a business term used to describe all of the efforts we put into various areas to draw people into what we ultimately want them to land on. As a blogger, all of your external efforts are primarily focused on drawing people to your blog itself. So, everything you do should ultimately be focused on drawing people in toward reading the posts you are posting and exploring the rest of the content that resides on your website.

You can do this through social media, paid advertisements, word of mouth, collaborations, contests, and even through business cards, flyers, and other in-person platforms that allow you to connect with your audience. Ultimately, anything that can help you drive traffic back toward your blog is a positive practice.

However, there are some things you need to consider. Primarily, you want to be focusing your efforts entirely on those that are returning great results. If you are putting effort into bringing people in and a certain method is not returning positive results, or the results are not worth the amount of investment it takes to get those results, then you likely want to cut that effort out. Instead, you can move toward focusing your energy on areas where the return on your time and financial investments are high.

Build an Online Presence

The biggest way to drive traffic to your blog is through having an online presence. Building your blog as a brand and then showing up online in various areas is a great way to ensure that you are interacting with your audience. This is how you can get in front of them on a regular basis, engage with your audience, connect with them more personally than a strictly blog-based presence allows for, and ultimately put your content in front of these people in the end. As you know, the entire purpose is to drive them back to your website.

Which social media websites you focus on will largely depend on who your target audience consists of. Facebook is generally a great place to start as nearly you're your audience exists on Facebook. However, determining whether Twitter, Instagram, YouTube, or other channels are going to be worthwhile or not will depend on where your audience hangs out the most. You can usually figure this out quickly through an internet search. I would provide you with a list, but the places where people hang out online is regularly changing and, therefore, it would be hard for that list to remain consistent or accurate for long. Instead, it is best if you take a look and pay attention to the current stats based on when you are starting your blog or when you are looking to take it to the next level.

When you are building an online presence, treat your social media as both a separate entity from your blog and a driving force for your blog. So, not every post should be specifically about your blog posts and topics you have talked about on your blog. Instead, post-organic content loaded with great information, interesting topics, humor, and attractive or funny pictures that will get your audience paying attention. The more that you interact with them, the better this will be for your traffic.

Your online presence will rely on three things: consistency, targeted content, and engagement. You should be posting at least three times a week, though daily is typically better. This keeps you relevant, at the top of the newsfeed, and regularly being exposed to the opportunity for people to see you and engage with your content. Then, you need to make sure that the content you are posting is actually stuff that people want to engage with. It should be interesting or attractive in some form so that it allows for people to truly want to get involved and start communicating with you, or at least liking and/or sharing your content. Then, when people do communicate with you through your social media platforms, be sure to comment back! Chat with them, show that you see them, and ultimately create a back-and-forth form of engagement so that your audience knows that you appreciate them and their loyalty. People who engage back with their audience are known to get far more loyalty and engagement to begin with, so this is definitely something you need to pay attention to. Regular engagement in this way will mean that every time you post a new blog post, you are more likely to drive people to your site through your social media as a result of the loyalty you have established.

Seek to Network with Others

When it comes to blogging, you do not have to be in a dog-eat-dog world. What that means is, you are not required to "hold your own" and stay completely in competition with other blogs in your niche. In fact, networking can be one of the most powerful moves that you make. When you put your name out there and get into the eyes of other bloggers, you open up a major potential for you to be further shared around. Because you begin to develop a relationship with these bloggers, they are more likely to refer people to your content when they see stuff that you've posted that they feel their audience will resonate with. The same should go in reverse, too. When they send people your way and support your growth, do the same for them! Network, and expand your audience.

In addition to simply chatting about each other's presence, networking allows you to open up the opportunity for collaborations. Collaborations in the blogging world mean posts that are done by two or more bloggers to provide even greater value for each of your unique audiences. If collaborations don't make sense or work for you, you can also use guest posting features as an opportunity for you to expand your network, and your reach. Opening up your blog for guest posters, or featuring on someone else's blog means that you both get the opportunity to cross-promote to each other's audiences. This means that you expand your reach and more people will begin to know who you are.

Networking in the blogging field is actually an incredible asset to have. Bloggers tend to band together to form a sort of community, and this community leads to each person within the community growing more successfully as a result of the shared support and promotion. By building a community of your own within the blogging industry with the help of other bloggers, you allow this form of cross-promotion and collective growth to take place. Naturally, this means great things for your own blog.

Consider Paid Promotions

While they are absolutely not necessary and are not ideal for someone with zero audiences, paid promotions can hold great value for those who already have a basic audience. When you know who your audience is, your growth through promotions is a lot easier to create.

The key to paid promotions is that you have to know who you are targeting in your advertisements. If you have not yet found your "spot" in the blogging world, then you have yet to actually discover exactly who your audience consists of. The reality is that in most cases, what we think our audience will be and who they actually are can vary. For that reason, you do not want to be wasting any of your valuable income on ads that are unlikely to effectively reach your target audience and gain you any form of return. Instead, you want to wait until you have an audience that is already creating some form of engagement and giving you feedback.

Once you have developed a clear basis for this analytics, however, you can begin using paid advertisements as an opportunity to promote your blog. In the beginning, start smaller until you begin to understand which advertisements work the best. Then, you can start investing more into paid advertising. When done properly and implemented at the right times, paid advertising can certainly be a valuable asset to growth. In fact, many people swear by it. The great thing about paid advertising is that one single advertisement can reach many, many people outside of your existing audience. This somewhat automates your growth and increases your growth ratios exponentially, if done properly.

Still, I can't stress enough that you should not invest in paid promotions until you have a fairly consistent audience in place. Once you do, begin looking at Google AdWords and various social media advertising platforms to provide you with the best opportunity to reach your audience. Ideally, you want to promote on the same social media platforms where you already get your highest levels of engagement. This is because this clearly proves that this is where a large amount of your audience hangs out and that you are more likely to get a great return here.

Chapter 8

Monetize Through Sponsored Content

The next popular way to monetize your blog is through sponsored content. This becomes more popular as your blog grows, as sponsors are typically looking for an active, proven, and loyal following in their bloggers. Once you have developed a consistent audience that is rapidly growing, you can begin working toward getting sponsored content deals. The following guidelines will help you understand how to land your deals, selecting which deals to go through with, and how the deal itself actually works.

When to Start Looking for Sponsorships

The best time to start looking for sponsorships is when you begin reaching a consistent following of a few thousand people. Ultimately, it depends on the specific company that you are looking to get a sponsorship with. However, the more followers and unique page visitors you have per month, the better. This is another reason why monitoring your analytics is valuable: it helps you know when to start looking for sponsorships, and it helps you know exactly what you are pitching when you pitch sponsor opportunities to companies.

Ideally, you want to have a minimum of 5,000 followers and unique page viewers on your website before you begin looking for sponsorship deals with smaller, startup companies. When you reach 10,000 and higher, you can begin looking for mature companies that are still fairly small in size. These would be mature, independent companies, for example, that have an established following but that are not mass corporations. If you want to start producing sponsored content for massive corporations, you will need upward of 100,000 followers. So, essentially, the more followers and unique page views you get per month, the larger your deals will become. The larger your deals are, the more money you will get paid per post.

Landing Sponsorship Deals

Getting sponsorship deals happens in two ways. Early on, it generally starts with you reaching out to companies. Later, you will likely find that companies start reaching out to you. Let's talk about early on, first.

Landing your sponsorship deals will start with you taking your analytics and approaching smaller companies. You want to approach small companies that reflect the unique industry you are writing for, and that sell products or services that your visitors would be most interested in. Then, you want to ask them if they would be interested in having a sponsored post on your website. Often, they will want to know more about you and your analytics before they consider agreeing. However, as long as your analytics support their cause, most smaller companies will be happy to do a sponsored post.

You should note that these posts will be worth a smaller amount. You may only make a couple of hundred dollars or less per post in the beginning. This is okay. The idea is that you are getting started and that you are getting used to these sponsorship deals.

As you begin growing in size and popularity, you can begin approaching more mature companies. Often, these companies will have professional channels of communication. You should always be sure to honor these channels, as this is what shows your professionalism. Since you are a business approaching another business, you need to ensure that you are viewed from a professional point of view. If you are unsure about who to ask, where, or how, you can always contact them and ask for directions on this information. In many cases, they are happy to provide you with information back.

Always make sure that you approach companies with professionalism. Do not pitch to them like you are trying to get something from them. Instead, pitch to them with authority, asserting what you have to offer to them so that they know that you realize how important the sponsorship is for them, as well as for you. Early on, you want to show that you have an intention to create an equal give-and-take partnership that will benefit your mutual audience, rather than coming off as though you are simply trying to earn a quick extra buck.

How to Ensure the Deal Is Good?

Once you start landing sponsorship deals, you need to be sure that you know how to look over the deals. Not every deal is a good one, and, therefore, you should not automatically assume that it is proper to say yes to any and every deal that comes your way. Instead, you need to make sure that you are looking them over and that they actually are a good deal.

Here is what you need to look for when you are ensuring a deal with a sponsor is good:

Your Expectations. If you have expectations going into the sponsorship such as getting free stuff to test for your audience or being paid, you need to be clear on this from the beginning. The company you are entering a sponsorship with should be willing to agree to these terms, assuming they are reasonable based on what you are offering them in return.

- ❖ Their Expectations. This is where you have to be extra cautious. When you sign a sponsorship agreement with some sponsors, there is a clause that states that you must give the item a positive review whether you like it or not. You should never take these deals. On the off chance that you dislike the product, you will be obligated to lie to your audience. If you get caught lying, your audience will lose trust in you, and, therefore, you will lose loyalty. This will have a highly negative impact on your bottom line. You should also consider how many times they want you to post and what you can or cannot say about the company itself. Some companies are fairly free and open with this, but others can get very specific and controlling. Be sure that you are completely aware of what you are getting into before you agree to any terms.
- ❖ Payment Method. Assuming you are getting paid for your sponsorship, you should know exactly how the payment is going to work. You should know when it will be released, what conditions need to be met for it to be released, and how you will receive it. If you do not know this or the terms seem inappropriate or somewhat shady to you, avoid the deal.

It is important that you are always careful on your sponsorship deals with regard to the fine print. Never agree to anything before you know exactly what it is that you agree to. Remember, as a blogger, your readers' loyalty is what results in you getting paid. If you break that loyalty, you will ultimately reduce the amount of income you make. You need to put your readers first, which means always being honest and only backing up products and services that you genuinely believe in.

Sponsorships with Affiliate Deals

Affiliate deals are another form of income entirely, but they often link with sponsorship deals. We are going to discuss both right now so that you understand how these work.

When you get sponsored, many companies will offer you an affiliate link. This typically comes with an exclusive code or coupon that your audience can use to receive a discount with the company that has sponsored your post. This means that you get paid for the post as well as anytime someone purchases products or services with your code. This results in you getting double-paid.

These deals can result in you earning an incredible additional amount of income, so always be on the lookout for these opportunities. If you have more say in your deal, you can always suggest or request this to be a part of it, too.

Affiliate deals do not have to be tied to sponsors. Many other companies, such as Amazon, have affiliate programs that you can become a part of. These give you access to unique links, codes, and other tools that you are given to drive your audience to their pages. When your audience lands on their page and shops for something, you are then paid a commission for that. This can be a great way to maximize your income, so it is definitely worth looking out for!

Sponsorship Agencies

Like advertisement agencies, sponsorship agencies are like a one-stop shop for getting sponsorships. While this typically won't land you with major companies, it is a great way to get started with sponsorships. There are many agencies out there, and they are continually changing. For that reason, there are none that I can currently recommend that will continue to be valid for a long period of time. In general, however, they are fairly easy to find through a quick internet search. Once you have found one, make sure you look up reviews to confirm that it is legitimate. Then, you can go ahead and create an account. The agency will then walk you through getting set up with companies so that they can begin sponsoring your posts! This is a great way to get started and can help you in the outreach process to bring income in.

How You Get Paid

Getting paid through sponsorships varies. Most often, they will pay you through PayPal, as this is the easiest payment strategy that is globally accepted. You generally get paid prior to posting the agreed upon post. However, if you go through a sponsorship agency, the company may pay the funds to the agency. This means that they will be held in escrow until the company agrees that you have met the terms of your agreement. Then, the funds will be released to you, and you can withdraw them in whatever way is supported by the agency themselves.

Chapter 9

SCOUTING THE COMPETITION TO LEARN THE BEST MONETIZATION PRACTICES

Luckily for you, finding the monetization methods that will work for your blog isn't as difficult as it used to be. In the past, bloggers need to do trial and error for months before they can find the right monetization company that they can work with. It is common practice nowadays among website owners to look up the monetization practices of their competitors and copy the ones that may work.

In each advertising widget added to a website, there is usually an information button located in them. All ads by Google, for instance, will an encircled 'i' icon. You can click this button to learn more about the ad.

The same goes for most automated ads services like the native content advertising platforms Taboola and Outbrain. If you look in the bottom corner of their advertising boxes, you will see a link saying "Ads by Taboola" or "Sponsored content by Outbrain." You can learn about almost all the advertising publishing methods used by other websites by examining the advertising box.

Some types of ads though do not show these signs. These types of ads or promotional materials are designed to blend in with the rest of the content on the page. An example of this is the banner ads by affiliate networks.

These ads show up like small static image boxes on the website with no indication that they are actually advertising. It is only when you click these images when you realize that they are ads because it redirects you to a seller's landing page or an internet offer.

For these types of ads, you can learn their source simply by clicking on the ads or hovering the mouse over them and checking the lower left corner of your browser.

This will show you the link where the image will lead to. An affiliate link will usually include an affiliate id number in them.

If you are not sure about the best types of monetization methods that you should use for your content, take the time to scrutinize the websites of your competitors. Look into the different types of ads that they run in their website and the features that they use to make these ads stand out. Aside from the ads, also check if they are selling something or if they are offering their own services.

You should list down all possible advertising methods used by your competitors and decide whether they could also be applied to your website. Some of the ads that they are running may not be accessible to you. For instance, they may be running exclusive ads for one company.

They negotiated these ads and sold the advertising space. If they are running these types of ads, then you will not be able to copy the method unless you also find an identical company to advertise on your own website.

Chapter 10

ADVERTISING

Many of the aspiring bloggers think that they will simply generate money by running advertisements on their blogs. They believe that they will set up a blog, write a few posts, and can start earning a steady income. Isn't that the case with many of us?

Sadly, that's not what happens in the blogging world. How much money you can eventually generate from your blog depends on the traffic that your blog can attract. If you are able to generate just a small number of views per day, it won't help you much in generating income, because not many people would be interested in using your blog for advertising. Generally speaking, you require at least 10,000 page views per before you can think of attracting advertisers.

The networks and companies that can bring more lucrative income streams to you need an even higher number of views before they consider your blog for placing advertisements. The numbers vary among different niches, but yes, don't start looking for advertisements before hitting the milestone of 10,000 views per month.

Google AdSense

If you are looking to get advertisements for your blog, you simply can't ignore Google AdSense. Most of the bloggers start out with Google AdSense because it accepts a wide variety of niches and traffic levels. A slower blog will obviously make less money than the one with higher traffic, but Google AdSense does accept those that have lower traffic blogs as well. Moreover, there are some ad formats that are limited only for people with higher viewership counts.

Google AdSense is quite simple to use in comparison to many other ad networks. The disadvantage of using this is that Google charges a chunk of your advertising revenue as commission, which is as high as 32%.

The income you can earn through Google AdSense depends on the size and style of advertisements you use, the niche your blog belongs to, and the traffic your blog attracts. There are three different bid models that advertisers can use to pay for the space on your page. The cost-per-click model is the most common. In this model, you get a commission every time a visitor clicks on the ad, even if they don't go any further through the site.

There's also a cost per thousand impressions model, where you get paid per thousand ad views, even if the viewers don't engage with the ad. The third type is the cost per engagement model, where the advertiser pays you for each time a viewer completes a specified task, like watching a video or completing a survey.

Knowing all of this is valuable in gaining more insight into how AdSense works, but one disadvantage of using AdSense over more selective ad networks is that you don't get to control which kind of ad goes on your page. Google determines which one will work best given your niche and your traffic levels.

As Google AdSense makes money from how much you generate, they are likely to select the most suitable style and content that's going to make you the maximum income (so that their commission is also maximized), but ultimately, it's up to Google to select the ads and their format that are displayed on your blog. You can just control the size and placement of the ad, but not more than that.

Due to its ease of use and high potential of income generation, Google AdSense is the most popular choice of bloggers, particularly for those that are just starting out to use advertisements as a means of generating income.

Other advertising networks

There is a plethora of different ad networks available for bloggers, most of which will require a higher traffic level than Google AdSense. Many are very choosy such as Revcontent which hardly accepts 2% of the applicants. However, there are others that don't require a minimum traffic level, making them approachable for new bloggers.

For example, you can look into using BidVertiser, Clicksor, and BlogAds. Do your own research before signing up with any of the ad networks. Check out other sites that use it to see how the ads show up on their blogs. Also try to talk to other bloggers about their experience with the site, because they can give your insights into their experience.

Remember that there is a reason that the more exclusive ad networks offer restricted access. Bloggers using those networks can generate higher income. Your aim should be to become part of such a network as your traffic grows to maximize your income potential.

Direct advertisers

Ad networks play an important role in the overall working of the ad market. They are the middle-man. They find advertisers and arrange payment. For providing these services, they take a commission. If you can deal with the advertiser directly, all the money from the ad is yours. However, this means that you do all the hassle of finding advertisers and dealing with them yourself.

In any case, bloggers hardly find direct advertisers when they have just started the blog because most direct advertisers require higher traffic numbers as compared to ad networks before committing.

One situation in which direct advertising could work for a lower traffic blog is if you run a site aimed at a town or community. A small business owner might find it worth his while to advertise on a blog that only gets 5,000 page views per month if all 5,000 of those views are likely to be from potential customers. Although new blogs generally don't stand a chance to get e direct ads, you should consider them if an opportunity strikes.

Affiliate income

Apart from earning income from ad placements, you can generate affiliate income by promoting others' products on your site. This is another effective way to earn passive income. There is no need for producing goods or services. However, you can only earn affiliate income when your readers buy a product from your affiliate. The advantage of affiliate sales for a new blog is due to the fact that unlike advertising, it does not entirely correlate to the number of views.

The most popular affiliate program is offered by Amazon. It's easy to start with Amazon's affiliate program. The other advantage is that the site has a huge variety of products for sale, so it's easy to find a product that fits well with your niche. There are two ways of generating income from affiliate programs. Either you can use affiliate links like advertising and make them a passive element of your page, or you can review or promote them with a separate post.

Another advantage of affiliate programs is that you have control over which products you want to promote through an affiliate program. You should only promote products that are useful to your readers. This way you can earn your readers' trust and loyalty. You should also select products connected to your chosen niche.

Improving your ad revenue

As simple as it might sound, where you place the ads on a page can impact your readers' level of engagement with it and subsequently with how much money you can make from it. While banner ads at the top of the page are one of the more common advertising styles, this isn't necessarily the best place to position the ad to get reader interaction. Including the ad within the main space of your posts will increase your average clicks per visit.

While you may not know the companies that advertise on your site when you're using an ad network, if you sign up advertisers directly, you should support them whenever possible. This doesn't necessarily mean writing "advertorials" (posts specifically dedicated to promoting advertisers) unless doing so would feel natural and organic to your blog, but you can engage with them in other ways without diminishing the integrity of your site.

Tweet to your advertisers from time to time. Know what they're up to and if they're releasing a new product or have an upcoming event that your readers would benefit from knowing about, be sure to share that information. Anything you can do to increase your value from the advertiser's perspective will only help you to bring in more revenue.

Blogger success story: Daniel Scocco

Daniel Scocco is best-known for running the site DailyBlogTips.com. At this point, Scocco is more focused on his software company and his online marketing training course rather than overseeing the day to day workings of his blog. Though he does some of the writing himself, he also employs a staff of paid writers and brings other bloggers in for guest posts.

He's grown his blog to the point that it generates a large amount of passive income for him, letting him focus on his other income streams. In a recent year, Scocco was able to make around $100,000 from Google AdSense alone, proving it's possible to make a living wage using AdSense—if you're willing to put in the work to build the site.

Chapter 11

Affiliate marketing

Many bloggers start trying to monetize and give up, leaving behind a trail of failed efforts. That's why you need to be constant and patient.

As I have already explained, you should start your blog with a clear segmentation in mind, focus on developing creative content, and apply a strategy to draw readership to your blog using the best tools in the market. You will definitely need to gain social media expertise for sharing your blog thus increasing your authority, visibility, reputation, and traffic. Once your traffic builds up, you would have to create an emailing list with an effective strategy, using once again the available tools. And now, the next step is to use affiliated products as a monetization option.

We are close to the last step. And I want you to understand this step clearly since affiliate products represent an excellent chance for monetization if the right strategies are applied.

The relevance of marketing affiliation can be exemplified with this statistic figure: during 2016, the affiliation market alone generated one billion dollars in the US; and it's expected that by 2020, the affiliate marketing investment alone will generate well over 6.8 billion dollars.

These numbers show the growth of the affiliate marketing trend which is why it

makes sense to consider offering affiliate products as a way to achieve monetization.

If you haven't done it because you've never heard about it, or because you think it's too complicated, then pay close attention because during the next couple of pages I'll show how you can easily implement this technique.

What is Affiliate Marketing?

It is one of the most effective ways to monetize when you don't have a product or service of your own to offer through your eBook. In fact, it is a good way to go, even if you do have a product or service since you can switch between your own products and affiliated ones.

Using affiliated products to sell on your blog is nothing more than recommending third party products, tools, or services through the advertiser's web. If you are able to convince your readers to buy the affiliate product that you've recommended on your blog, then you earn a sale's commission.

So, using affiliated products is basically using your blog to talk about those products and driving your readers to the advertiser's website for making the purchase.

It's a win-win situation. The advertiser wins, you get to earn a commission, and the user wins because they get a product that solves a particular need or problem.

Affiliate marketing allows the use of an affiliated link or code: a link that lets the advertiser know that a user has visited their site and made a purchase from your blog.

It's important to know this technique's mechanism, so you can implement it perfectly. This mechanism is effective because if the user accesses the advertiser's website through your blog but doesn't buy the product right then, you still have a chance at getting a sale's commission if the reader buys the product later.

This is possible because when the reader visits the page from your blog's affiliate link, a cookie is enabled, which is a code that allows the user to be identified and leaves a trail that shows where the user came from.

Regardless of whether a user buys a product or not, a cookie is still stored in the browser that identifies him if he returns. As a general rule, the lifespan of cookies is 30 days, although this depends on the advertiser's settings. This entails that if they purchase the product within a month of clicking at your affiliate link, you get to earn a commission off that sale and this makes this a very effective method of monetization.

Keys to making affiliate marketing work

Using affiliate products will give you good results only if you use it the right way. Given below is a useful outline for using this method of monetization for your blog.

- You need a loyal community

Using affiliate product will only work if you have a community of loyal readers. Why? Because you're recommending third party products, so you need them to have enough respect for your opinion to actually buy those.

So, your ideal reader must trust you and should accept your recommendations; they need to know that you have a genuine interest in their problems and know how to solve them.

In order for your audience to trust you, you need to provide high value with each email. Remember I said that you shouldn't be cheap?

This way, your readers will thank you for your generosity by trusting you and what you recommend. Focus on bringing useful content through your posts, help with their needs, and grant them access to high-quality content so they can benefit from reading it.

Create a connection in which your willingness to help is palpable.

Your blog must develop topics that you're passionate about so you'll write with pleasure. You have to believe you're blogging to help others; monetization will be the result of your commitment to that mission.

Your audience will trust you only when you have contributed to their lives; and after you earned their trust, you need to keep doing it.

Starting your blog with attempts at monetization is a crass mistake. If people don't know you, they won't buy from you or accept your recommendations; you may only make an occasional sale. But believe me, building a loyal audience and earning their trust is worth the effort. Only then will you be able to offer affiliate products; the end results will make all the journey worthwhile.

As you earn your reader's trust, you get to know them better and learn more about their interests, urgencies, language, searches, and much more. And all the information you acquire will help you optimize your sales strategies.

- Offer only those products that you have bought or would buy

You have a trusting community. Now it's time for action. To get good results through affiliate product sales, you need to make sure that you're offering something that will give them good results.

Your audience will accept your recommendation because you've established yourself as an authority on the matter. So, if you recommend a particular tool, they will buy it because they know that if you're talking about it, then it must be good.

That trust must not be broken. Don't recommend products that you don't believe in, even if you've been offered good money for it by a sponsor. You might make good sales, but you're losing what you have worked so hard to build, and that is a faithful audience.

The best way to decide whether an affiliate product is a good product to recommend to your audience is to ask yourself if you would do it if there were no reward. That's how you care for the reputation that you have built and make sure that your monetization lasts.

If the product that you choose to recommend is useful, you'll be getting loyal buyers and evangelists; people who buy the product, try it and recommend it to others as they had a positive experience. The next time you recommend a product, they'll buy it without hesitation. You'll get commissions off the sales of the affiliate products because you're doing it the right way.

When you find a product that you would recommend only for the money and not for its value and effectiveness for your audience, then it's better to avoid the temptation.

Promote only what you would buy or have bought. If the product is merely interesting for you, share with them that you find it appealing. Some users may try it, knowing that you are not recommending the product, but merely showing your interest. They may even be the ones who share their experience and critique on whether it's a product worth buying or not.

Respect your audience, and you'll reap the benefits. This is the basic principle for smart, long-term monetization.

- Before recommending a purchase, offer as much information as you can

You may think that if the goal is to get users to click the link to enable the cookie that will link that sale to you, the best option would be to present the link right away.

That logic, however, is deeply flawed. Many blogs make that very mistake. You access the blog and see the huge button to buy your affiliate product right away, causing them to feel as if they're being cornered. That's like saying, "You have no other choice, so you better click on this button!"

It's not a good idea to leave your readers without a choice. Cornering them will not force them to click on the button, but they might leave your blog right away and never come back.

If you provide your reader with valuable information about the product, he will have a chance to find out what it is that you're offering and if you stick to your segmentation and what you know about your ideal reader from your constant interaction with them through email marketing, then the chances are that they will click on the link and explore the product that you're offering before deciding to buy.

If you place the button at the beginning of the post, without giving them enough information, you're losing control of that sale. You're relinquishing your influence and your ability to help them make decisions. You're relying on luck to make that sale.

You might say, "Russell, but Amazon has buttons at the top of the page to present products."

The answer is clear and simple: Amazon has worked tirelessly to build a reputation and has become a platform with unquestionable authority. And even so, you don't press the button until you have checked all the information related to the product, the seller, and the shipment, right?

So, come up with a post for each affiliate product and include as much information as you can. In this post, you will describe the features of the product and the benefits that it may bring to your ideal readers. You can also include a video showing how that product works. You don't need to produce it; it would be enough to find a YouTube video for this purpose. But if you do have the time, ability, and creativity to create your own video, then I advise that you do so.

You can also incorporate a Q&A section to your post. Since you understand your audience, you may guess what might hold them back from buying that product. So, be proactive and help them overcome any objection that they might have to make that purchase.

Another possible element to include in your post are opinions from current users of that product. That, together with your opinion about it, will help them make a decision.

Follow this advice and the sale will not be left to chance; on the contrary, you'll be increasing the chances of getting your audience to buy, therefore generating a bigger income.

Types of affiliate marketing

These are the following two types of affiliate marketing available:

- ❖ Affiliate platforms
- ❖ Direct affiliate programs

They present a slight but important variation.

- Affiliate platform

It represents a system of affiliates that are indirectly managed. It's a series of web platforms that act as mediators between your blog and the advertisers.

When you sign up on this type of platform, you access a variety of advertisers and their products. You get to promote those products to earn a commission.

To use affiliate platforms, you need to take the following steps into account:

Crawley Library

Self Service Receipt for Borrowed Item

Name: *****5139

Title: Blogging, a 6-Figure Strategy

Item: 202120373

Due Back: 26/06/24

Total Borrowed: 1
05/06/2024 13:59:37

Sign up: Complete the registration form. They usually ask the URL of the website where you'll be promoting their products. Your request must be approved before you begin promoting.

Find advertisers: When you have signed up, and your account is approved, you can search for advertisers of the products you wish to promote. The sites offer a search tool and the advertisers are categorized which makes the search easier.

Register: Once you find the advertiser whose product you'd like to promote, you should register with them. You have to wait until your blog has been checked and the advertiser approves your request. If they do, you'll get a link to add to your blog.

Monitor Your performance: The platform will provide a control panel that will give you access to statistics. This will let you know if your link is working and if you're earning commissions.

I can recommend the following affiliate platforms:

- ❖ Tradedoubler

- ❖ Zanox
- ❖ Webgains
- ❖ Affilinet
- ❖ Commision
- ❖ Junction
- ❖ Shareasale
- ❖ Public ideas

The important thing is to use the same platform for all the products that you promote. This is because you'll get better chances of raising enough money to make a withdrawal.

These platforms give you the chance to withdraw money via your bank account or PayPal account when you have reached a particular minimum that they assign. If you promote from different platforms, it'll be harder to reach that minimum in all of them.

If you promote two or more products from the same affiliate platform, then your chances of reaching that minimum increase.

Besides, the larger the income, the better treatment you'll get from the affiliate platform. You'll earn better commissions and personalized support among other benefits.

Now, I'll describe the second option to monetize through affiliate products.

• Direct affiliate programs

Some advertisers prefer to manage their own affiliate programs. So, you don't need to sign up on an affiliate platform to earn a commission off the sales of their products.

Using this system, you can earn a commission directly. There is no platform managing and tracking the sales, so in many cases, the commissions are higher.

I'll introduce three platforms that use this system and provide the opportunity to sell affiliate products directly.

Booking: This platform allows their products to be sold through direct affiliate marketing since they have a self-managed affiliate program. In fact, you can sell their affiliate products through the Public Ideas platform.

Amazon: You can earn a commission through the recommendation of any product on sale on the platform.

eBay: Its affiliate program runs on the same mechanism as Amazon's.

To operate with direct affiliate systems, you need to sign up just like you would on any affiliate platform. You can find clear instructions on these advertisers' websites. When you sign up, you can look up the affiliate links to use on your blog and start monetizing.

Affiliate products are a good way to start monetizing if you don't have

products of your own. But, bear in mind that monetization doesn't happen a week or two after you start a blog.

You need to invest time and money in positioning your blog and creating an emailing list. Only then will you be able to start monetizing. You also have to be serious about investing to generate a higher income through your blog. Remember that if you follow each step, monetization is a guaranteed outcome.

In this chapter, I have covered the basic aspects to start monetizing through affiliate products. However, there's yet another option left.

Don't stop here, go onto the next step, and you'll be ready to capitalize your blog to the fullest.

Chapter 12

Facebook Marketing

Facebook is huge. As the biggest social networking site on the planet, it has more than 2.20 billion dynamic clients, 66% of whom sign in every day.

Facebook went from being obscure, barely 10 years prior, to having billions of individuals utilizing it daily. Will Facebook be doomed to failure like other social media sites in the past? I think not. Facebook is digging in for the long haul. Also, with such an expansive client base, overlooking Facebook truly isn't a smart idea, especially if you are serious about online marketing.

You can target your ideal market using Facebook steadily. The analysis is: how would you gain more clients with your ads with Facebook?

Fortunately, the Facebook promoting stage enables you to zero in and indicate the kind of individuals you're searching for. You can focus by area, socioeconomics, interests, and significantly more.

In this guide, I'll show you the rudiments of generally-accepted methods to utilize Facebook, further boosting your advantage. The guide is for the quick learner who needs an opening to showcasing their business on the world's biggest social media site.

Who's On Facebook?

Facebook began as an informal community for undergrads, but in any case, at this point, about everybody with a website uses it. The minimum age for using Facebook is 13, and it can be safely assumed that it as is being used by all other age groups.

Facebook doesn't openly discharge information on their most prominent age groups, yet a study by Pew demonstrated that person to person communication is most prevalent with the 18-29 age groups. Its prominence diminishes with age. It is also used by those in the 65 and above groups.

I can guarantee that enough number of people belonging to your target age group are using Facebook.

How Might You Market on Facebook?

Facebook has three tools (pages, ads, and social affairs) that can be used by anyone. All of these choices have their very own market, and they can be joined for more significant reach for your customer needs.

Pages

Facebook pages resemble profiles, for associations, affiliations, and open figures markets.

Clients can "Like" a page, which means that they'll naturally get posts from that page in their newsfeed. Be that as it may, with the end goal to see the posts each time they are included, you have to tap the alternative to see posts first. Something else of importance, it's imaginable you won't see the updates in light of the fact that Facebook needs Pages to help (burn through cash) posts for greater reach to users.

Users additionally have the choice to "Like" a page but not tail it. (Clients likewise can pursue a few profiles if they wish).

While profiles require a shared connection between friends, pages can be liked by anybody, and the page maker does not have to acknowledge a fan. They additionally don't have a limitation on the quantity of companions/fans they can have (in contrast to profiles, which are restricted to 5,000 friends).

Points of interest: Pages are free and simple to set up.

Hindrances: It can be difficult to get a solid footing and manufacture a fan base with a page.

Promotions

Facebook offers an awesome focus on publicizing. You can make promotions focused on explicit geographic regions, ages, instruction levels, and even the kinds of gadgets utilized for checking. Facebook, likewise, gives clients a chance to hide promotions they don't care for and "Like" a page appropriate underneath an ad.

Favorable circumstances: Ads have incredible focusing on target consumers.

Inconveniences: Ads can get costly, contingent upon your objectives.

Gatherings

Facebook groups are like discourse gatherings. However, they have extra highlights that show pages and profiles; you can use these groups to your advantage or even create one yourself (like a course of events). You can create a group identified with your industry or item contributions as an approach to contact potential clients.

Favorable circumstances: Groups are free and have elevated amounts of commitment.

Detriments: Groups can be extremely tedious and demanding to upkeep.

The Most Effective Method to Market with Pages

Facebook pages are the most effective and least demanding approach to begin marketing with Facebook.

To use the site is free, generally simple to set up (at any rate in their essential structures), and unimaginably adaptable. There are virtually no drawbacks, either.

Unfortunately, numerous organizations don't utilize Facebook to its maximum capacity, or even worse, utilize it ineffectively. The rules laid out in this book will enable you to abstain from committing those errors.

Profile Photo and Cover Image

Your profile photo ought to be your logo; it's as simple as that. The cover picture is an alternate story. It's genuinely up to you to pick what to put here. Some use photos of agents while others use luxurious HD premium photos and put their contact information in the cover picture. Pick a photo that will update your page and draw the eye of your visitors.

"About" Section

The "About" section should be put directly underneath your business logo. This is your chance to encourage anyone visiting your page what your business offers.

Ensure you put great information here, telling individuals what your organization does, for what reason you're extraordinary, and other fascinating points of interest. Set aside the time to compose this area explicitly for your Facebook gathering of people.

You can duplicate the content from the "About" page of your site or blog in case you're not sure what to put. Make sure to fill in the majority of your information under "Essential Info." You likewise might need to put your business address in this section if you have a physical store location.

Keep it neat and casual. An easygoing tone is the most suitable for Facebook.

Post Useful Information to Your Timeline

What you post to your timeline, what your put will appear in the news channels of everybody who has "Liked" your page, similarly as it does when you present something on your own profile.

Along these lines, guarantee what you're showing is profitable and draws in on your followers. Do whatever it takes not to post boundless updates about a comparable thing, and don't post unnecessary information that doesn't cater to your followers either.

Here are a few thoughts for the sorts of things you should post to your page:

- ❖ Connections to articles identified with your organization or your industry.
- ❖ Connections to your blog entries.
- ❖ Coupon codes for fans to get a good deal on your things.

New Thing Assertions

Make connections to your fans that they may discover as valuable.

Once more, ensure that your posts are prized. Likewise, don't post time and again every day, except if there's an uncommon occasion going on, or something new of importance to them.

Ask Your Fans Questions

Getting your fans to take a liking to your page is an incredible method to stir confidence and get them to trust you and see you as a leader in your field.

The questions you ask depend on your item and your specialty, yet asking open- inquiries more often than not gathers the best reactions.

Asking questions on another item thought or undertaking can be a decent method to convince your fans that you think about what they need. Getting a greater commitment to a post may likewise enable you to achieve the highest point of the Facebook News Feed.

Try not to Spam

Spam is one of the fastest ways to lose fans. In case you don't do anything to annoy them, yet convey limited time blurbs about your organization while never including anything of significant worth, at that point you will experience considerable difficulties getting and keeping fans. Before you post anything, inquire as to whether it genuinely increases the value of the discussion. If not, don't send it.

Concentrate Your Statistics and Results

Facebook Insights offer some extremely extraordinary inquiry for pages. Focus on them. For example, say you see a major flood in fans (or a drop off), see what you've posted lately, and assess whether you can make sense of an explanation behind the pattern. By then, post a more prominent measure of that kind of material (or less, on the off chance that you're losing fans).

Directed Advertising

Facebook advertising collects so much statistical data about its clients that it has an outstanding track record amongst other social media marketing sites on the web.

You can target customers based on practically anything you may discover in their profiles and additionally track your success with each quota.

Promotions can be kept running on for every impression or per-click basis. Facebook demonstrates to your followers what offers are for promotions like yours, so you can compare your offer with others in the same your industry. Similarly, you can set day by day tracking, so there's no danger of blowing your financial plan for ads.

Varieties of Facebook Ads

There are many different promotions you can do with Facebook. You can make advancements that direct to your Facebook page or to a site not on Facebook. You can make promotions to propel a Facebook event, complete with an RSVP associate. You can make advancements for compact application presents and application responsibility.

Clients Can Hide Your Ad

Facebook used to offer the choice to "Like" any ad on Facebook, but it is not the case any longer. Individuals can "Like" a post (if it's that type) or hide the promotion. After shutting a promotion, Facebook asks the client to determine the reason they don't like it. It's profitable data, giving understanding into why your promotions probably won't do.

Incredible Targeting Options

Facebook has probably the most incredible targeting options available on the web.

You can focus on anything that a client has on their profile. You may begin with key areas that are essential. You can indicate the city, postal district, area, or state. This works especially well for neighborhood organizations and businesses. You can choose socioeconomic factors such as relationship status, age, work environment, training (counting major and long stretches of participation), birthday, and others.

You also can target people based on their interests. For instance, you have a thing that is targeted at cricket fans. You could enter cricket in the Interests field. Or on the other hand, possibly you've written a book, and you're certain that individuals who like another specific book will like yours. You can simply write the book's title under "Interests," and you'll explicitly focus on those readers.

You even can concentrate on a private summary of customers. If you have an email list of areas on people that you want to target, you can use Facebook's advancements to target just those people. Along these lines, in case you keep up a SaaS business and have 200 people that show up on your "page" that appear, you can use their emails to target them with ads on Facebook.

Tweak Your Ads

The really fantastic thing about Facebook ads is that you can focus on promotions that can make distinctive advertisements for various groups. Staying better-focused on advertisements will accumulate better outcomes.

For example, if you're concentrating on football fans, you may make commercials for different gatherings. You could have one advancement expressly done for NFL fans, one at Seattle Seahawks fans, and another at Raiders fans, and a short time later, have those promotions presented just to people who have appeared for football, further boosting your advantage to lovers of those groups.

Then again, suppose you've focused on individuals dependent on their adoration for a specific book. You could specify that book in the promotion itself to make it bound to grab their eye.

Facebook isn't simply ground-breaking. It's adaptable. Regardless of what kind of organization you run, it has enough unique advertising alternatives that you can tailor your showcasing endeavors to accommodate your organization, your financial plan, and your time imperatives.

Indeed, it can set aside some opportunity to become more acquainted with the majority of its highlights. However, it's acceptable, despite a little work on your part. Facebook still is developing at a quick pace, and consistently, it turns into a more fundamental piece of online business with social media marketing.

It's likewise vital to make the most of current opportunities. For the occasion, businesses that are shrewd about Facebook ads still appreciate an early-adopter advantage.

Yet again, customary advertisers begin progressing into space, the rivalry will build, publicizing costs will rise, and clients will turn out to be a lot pickier.

On the off chance that Facebook is definitely not a present piece of your advertising effort, it ought to be. Put aside some time to gain an opportunity to grow your business, begin a couple of ads, and see what happens.

All these strategies work on Facebook, but you just have to get used to practicing how things work, once you do it, then it becomes easy to do, your business will skyrocket.

Chapter 13

MONITOR YOUR ANALYTICS

Since you are running your blog with the intention of making funds from it, you need to regard it as a business. As with any business, your analytics play a huge role in helping guide you through the process of growing your blog and maximizing your income and profitability. By paying attention to these important analytics, you give yourself the opportunity to discover where your biggest growth resides, how you can amplify that growth, and what strategies you need to enforce further to create the results that you desire. In this chapter, we are going to explore what your analytics are, how you can pay attention to them, and what they tell you in terms of where your growth potential lies.

What Are Analytics?

Analytics is like your "results." These are the statistics that show you how successfully (or not) a certain effort performed. Blog posts, social media posts, advertisements, and other outreach efforts are all gauged based on how well they have performed. By paying attention to these results, you can analyze the success of various strategies, and thus, you can locate where the maximum opportunity for success resides.

Your analytics are typically posted for you in the backend of your blog hosting platform on the backend of your social media managers and in other locations. Paying attention to these results can significantly boost your ability to know what you should do to maximize growth.

Logically, you want to do more of what gets you better engagement and results, and less of what doesn't. So, when you are paying attention to analytics, you want to be paying attention to both sides of the spectrum. Look at what people were most interested in, and what they were least interested in. Then, when you have, you can also pay attention to how these posts and outreach strategies differed and what that means for you. Ultimately, you want to take these as "lessons" that you can use to guide you through future outreach efforts.

Pay Attention to Popular Titles and Articles

The first thing you want to pay attention to when you are looking into your analytics is what was the most popular. You want to see what people clicked onto most, which titles earned the highest number of likes and shares, and where people were getting the most engaged. Paying attention to these posts is going to give you ample information on what people are interested in, what they want to see more of, and how you can tailor future content to serve your audience.

Since this is where the majority of your information will come from, some believe that you should go beyond going into each individual metric system attached to each account to monitor your analytics. I would have to agree.

You can do this by opening some form of document on your computer and begin posting the links to the content that performed the best as well as specific metrics. For example, how many hits the page got, how many likes or shares it got, how many people commented, and what platform it was posted on. You can also include information about how you promoted this content if you did. You should also jot down some form of notes outlining primary points associated with each post so that you can begin to recognize themes and trends in your popular titles and posts. This puts everything in one place so that it is easy to see where your success lies.

Collect Data to See What Exactly People Like

Like we discussed above, the idea is to get a very clear idea of what people like. As you are collecting your data, putting together trends and themes and following those is a great way to make sure that you are staying on top of everything and that you are learning the most that you can about what your followers like. This gives you the opportunity to see what it is that draws them in, to begin with.

When you know what draws people in, it becomes a lot easier to incorporate more of that in future content. This means that you can begin specifically tailoring your content, both through blog posts and outreach efforts such as on social media, for your audience. Through these efforts, it becomes a lot easier to post more of what your audience is likely to share and like. The more they engage, the better your outreach will perform. Then, as a result, your audience will begin to rapidly grow.

Be Sure to Consider What People Don't Like, Too

When you are collecting analytics, it is always important to consider both ends of the spectrum, too. This would be anywhere where posts don't perform well. Now, before you begin inspecting underperforming posts, it is important to know what an underperforming post actually looks like.

As you begin to post more content, you will likely notice that you have an average. For example, maybe your average engagement is something like 1000 viewers per post. So, a post that is performing exceptionally would be any post with more than, say, 1100 viewers, with more being even better. A post that would be underperforming, however, would be one with significantly fewer viewers than 1000. Say, 900 or less. When you find a post that has significantly fewer views than your average, it is important that you analyze this post, too.

When you analyze these underperforming posts, the goal is to understand why they performed poorly. What did you do differently with this post that resulted in it not performing as well? You want to identify what it was that resulted in people not being as drawn into it or as interested in it. This will help you ensure that you don't carry these ineffective strategies forward and potentially damage your growth by doing things your audience doesn't respond well to.

Understanding both ends of the spectrum allows you to do more of what your audience does like and less of what they don't like every single time. This is how you can maximize your viewership by making sure that you are paying close attention to what your audience wants and needs.

Post More Content That Will Earn Likes and Shares

Now that you know what you are looking for with regard to what your audience likes and dislikes, it's time to start creating more content that they are going to respond well to! Consider your analytics direct feedback toward what your audience wants you to talk about and share. Then, with that knowledge, you simply agree! Talk about the topics they enjoy, use titles that they respond well to, post in areas that they tend to spend time in, post at the right time of day, and follow all of the trends that you have discovered in your analysis. By following these strategies, you can ensure that you are going to have major success in the long run.

Never Stop Checking Your Analytics

Before we end the discussion on analytics, we need to get clear on one very important thing. There is never a time in your blogging career where you should stop performing analytic checks. Every week or every month, whichever works best for you, you need to be checking analytics. This is how you can ensure that you are staying on top of trends and themes. As you likely already know, trends and themes change rapidly. Staying on top of your analytics allows you to be ahead of the curve.

If you ever stop checking on your analytics, you can almost certainly guarantee that your success is going to begin to fall. This is because you are no longer listening to your audience and producing content that directly relates to what they have "asked" for. As a result, they are no longer tuning in to what you are saying.

If you are only blogging for fun, then you can stop checking analytics and follow whatever trend it is that you want to. However, if you want to blog to earn an annual salary of six figures per year, you need to stay focused on your analytics. These act as a form of a compass to guide you in the proper direction, and ignoring them may result in you losing out on major success and therefore major profitability!

Chapter 14

INCOME STREAMS

Once you have successfully created your website, all that is left to do is to start actively monetizing it in as many different ways as possible. It is important to keep your expectations realistic at this point and to remember that just as starting your blog was lots of work, so too will be monetizing it. However, it will be worth all your efforts, and if you persevere, then passive income awaits.

Additionally, you need to be aware that getting a full-time paycheck from a blog at this point is going to be a full-time job. Each new post that you create takes you one step closer to a passive income stream. However, slow and steady wins the race. Early on, it is crucial for your blog to have plenty of new content on a regular basis, not just constant advertising. You need to build your readers trust first before you start trying to make money.

Create the right type of content: When it comes to successfully monetizing your blog, the first thing that you are going to need to do is to create the kind of content that is in your niche or sub-niche so that your readers are genuinely interested. If you are already very active in the niche in question, then this should be relatively easy; otherwise, you will want to start by doing research on the most popular blogs on the topic as a way of learning not just what those who are interested in the topic are most passionate about but also how they express themselves, what types of slang and jargon they use, and the types of things that are important to them both personally and in the workplace. Additionally, spending plenty of time on these sites will provide you with the opportunity to look for gaps in their coverage that you will then be able to exploit on your site.

Once you know what type of content you should be providing, the next thing you need to think about is how you will put a personal spin on it. Regurgitating standard information will get you nowhere, which is why you are going to need to create a niche-specific persona if you aren't naturally a person your niche would turn to for advice. This persona shouldn't be a stereotype but, instead, needs to be someone that a large portion of your audience will relate to. Once your audience can relate to you, you will find that it is much easier to sell them things.

Finally, once you know what you are going to write about and what slant you are going to put on things, all that is left to do is to get writing. Once your site goes live, you are going to want to post multiple pieces of new content every day to ensure that you force people to get in the habit of checking your site regularly, which means you are going to need a log of 50 blog posts or so to ensure that you have time to keep up the flow. If that seems like too much writing, you might want to reconsider your choice of passive income.

Start with monetization basics: No matter what platform you use, you will have the ability to sell ad space. Normally, you are going to be able to get a few pennies every time that someone clicks on an ad, and the most popular way is to enroll with Google Adsense so that relevant ads are placed without you having to go out and find individual advertisers. Depending on the amount of traffic that your site sees, you could be getting up to $0.50 every time someone clicks on the ad.

Ads are going to be the easiest way for you to make money on your site, but they require lots of page views to be profitable on their own truly. The best way to increase your revenue stream right off of the bat is by joining what is recognized as an affiliate marketing program that is going to allow you to have a more targeted form of advertising. The most common affiliate advertiser is Amazon, and anyone can sign up to be an Amazon affiliate. Once you join, all you need to do is to choose products that your niche is interested in, write positive reviews of the products, and include a special link that will be provided to you to let your readers buy the product if they are so inclined. Each purchase that is made from your link puts money directly into your pocket in an amount that is proportional to the cost of the item in question.

If you plan on going down this route, it is important only to choose products that you have first purchased and can genuinely vouch for. As a blogger, all you have is your name and your reputation, and if you tarnish that reputation by selling cheap products, then you will lose readers faster than you can possibly imagine. Likewise, it is important that these types of product reviews are only one of the types of content that you provide if you want people to stick around in the long term. A ratio of 10 percent advertising-based post is typically considered acceptable by many bloggers.

Paid Content: If you regularly offer useful information on your blog, then paid content is a good method for you to consider, especially should the information that you are putting out there help your readers make money. To proceed down this path, all you need to do is make a separate members-only section of your site that allows paid access to various types of content.

- ➢ eBooks: You can put all of your top tips or put something new altogether in an eBook, and it will be a reader-friendly way to not only get

your content offline but also package that content.
- ➢ White papers: These are similar to eBooks, but they are going to be smaller and more technically written.
- ➢ Phone calls: If you are offering a service, phone calls are a good way to sell that advice; have your readers pay for the phone call and any other consulting you may be offering.
- ➢ Miniguides: Short guides can be a helpful series that you can sell to your readers on how they can do things.
- ➢ Tutorials: Video tutorials can be comprised of the same material as the guides, and you will have the ability to compile tutorials together on what you are an expert at.
- ➢ Podcasts: They may be a rare gift to your readers, and if you have a loyal reader base, they may be willing to pay to be able to hear any additional advice that you have to offer or just to be able to keep up with your blog whenever they are on the go.
- ➢ Videos: This is another good addition. Some readers will be willing to pay for it because it

makes it easier for them to read your blog without having to stare at your blog and read the words.

Physical products

If you have the ability to create things with your hands, then you may want to sell them on your blog as well! If you have a website where all of the products that you have to offer can be seen, place that on your blog so that people are able to go to your website and see what it is that you have. There are websites such as Etsy that allow for you to sell your products to people without having to be fearful of if you are going to get the money because you are going to get the money before you ever send the product out.

However, with physical product, you are going to want to be careful about what you are putting on your blog. If your product is for those who are 18 years old or older, then you are going to want to hide the link to the website because you do not want anyone who is not supposed to have the product get their hands on it.

Also, keep in mind that what is legal in your state may not be legal in another. So, before you ship any products out, you need to ensure that you are not shipping them to a state where it is illegal to have that product.

Begging

No one likes begging, but no one likes someone who is being sneaky either, so be upfront about wanting to earn money with your blog. But, be polite when you are asking. The people that actually value what you are writing about are going to be more willing to show their support in order to help you keep going and be successful.

- PayPal: It offers a button that you can put on your blog that is going to allow your readers to give you donations.
- Amazon Honor System: This is similar to PayPal's donation button, but it is through Amazon.
- Patreon: With this, you are going to be using a platform that is based on crowdfunding. By using Patreon, you can get donations for your

posts on a regular basis or per post if you prefer. Using Patreon, you are going to be able to get monthly donations as well as set a monthly goal.

➢ Tangible objects: Some readers want to give gifts that they made to their favorite people. To enable people to do this, set up a PO Box that is dedicated to letters and anything else that people may want to send you.

RSS Ads

For more specialized advertising, RSS is going to allow bloggers to monetize their feeds. But, remember that readers do not want to see their favorite blog overtaken by ads, regular or RSS. Restrict the number of RSS ads that are on your blog.

➢ Pheedo Inc: This RSS platform offers an interactive trigger as well as video options.
➢ Feedvertising: This is part of text link ads that will be embedded in the RSS feed.
➢ CrispAds: This platform is going to focus the ad network so that you are able to place the

ads into entries that are going to show up on your site as well as the feeds.

- FeedBurner Inc: The ads are going to be embedded in the RSS feed while featuring high-quality advertisers such as Best Buy.
- FeddM8: Your blog is going to be mobile ready while having the relevant mobile advertising embedded.

Chapter 15

Start Selling from Day One

You need to have motivation when you are selling anything, and that includes when you are selling your blog. Your blog is a product! Advertisers want a space of it, and if you are selling advertising space, then you are going to want to have the motivation to sell it.

When you are using things such as AdSense, the price for the amount of room that the advertiser wants is going to be set by the application that you are using. But, you can also sell ads to other people.

Take, for example, your favorite book blog. When you go to their blog, it is highly likely that you are going to see book covers of books that were just released or are about to be published on the sides of the page with their posts in the middle and their navigation bar at the top.

Now, if you will, think about not putting those covers and countdowns up without selling that space to the author for a predetermined amount of time, like AdSense does. In doing this, the owner of the blog is offering the space on their blog to the author so that their book gets out there for other people to know about.

In doing this, you are going to have to be fair about the price that you are offering the space to your "client" for without charging them so much that they do not want to advertise with you or too little that you are harming your own profits.

But, how do you get these customers to your blog? You become motivated! You go out and contact people that you know would benefit from buying space on your blog. And, it does not have to be just advertising, it can be allowing them to post on your blog, doing interviews, so on and so forth. It is your blog, and you are going to be able to sell it however you want.

Just do not think that you are going to be able to do this without putting in the needed amount of work. A useful way to think of it is that your blog is an object that you are trying to sell. Do not sell your entire blog, but do not hold back on what possibilities there are in marketing your blog. It is all going to start from the very first day that you start your blog.

While this may seem a bit silly because you are not going to have a big readership when you are first starting out, you are going to attract readers with the ads and people that you invite to your blog.

You do not need to try and overdo it though. If someone is hesitant about buying space from you, do not harass them about it, and do not talk bad about them. That is going to not only drive off potential business, but it is also going to turn readers off. Besides, doing this gives you no class and will create a bad name for yourself so that no one wants to work with you. On top of not harassing them, you are not going to want to let them forget either if they showed interest in possibly using your blog. Without driving them off, you are going to want to ask them if they are interested or let them know if you are offering any specials on selling out your blog.

One of the best things that you can do to sell on your blog is to have established trust with your readers because they are going to be able to bring you more readers, and those readers can be people who end up wanting to spend money on advertising on your blog.

Going back to our previous model with the book blog, they are trying to get authors, editors, or whoever else to advertise on their site. Now, in selling, it is easy to go with the first person that is going to offer you money or give you money because that is just going in your pocket. However, it is not going to make much sense to sell to a person that is advertising makeup products when it comes to a book blog, does it?

The people that you invite to your blog to do posts get advertising space; whatever it is that you are selling, they need to be people that match up with the niche that you have chosen. If your readers find irrelevant material on your page, you could lose them.

Chapter 16

Branding your Blog and other Online Platforms

If you are serious about your blog and where it's going in the near future, and you have long-term goals for your blog, then you might need to consider properly branding your blog right from the start.

Naming your blog according to your niche

When you are selecting a name for your blog, I recommend that you brainstorm a name that is in line with the topic of your blog. For instance, if your blog is in the niche of parenting, then choose a name which relates to parenting. People should be able to tell that it is a parenting blog just by looking at the name.

An advantage of selecting such a name is that it will attract people to visit your blog. When they come across your blog name, as shown in your domain name, they would be motivated to visit it. It would attract them if they are looking for a particular niche. They would be able to tell immediately that it pertains to what they are searching.

When they visit your blog and like it (hopefully), they could end up liking and following your blog and what could be better than that for you?

Using Your Own Name As The Brand Name. Some bloggers just use their names as the name of their blog instead of thinking of a name pertaining to their niche. Sometimes, this can help bloggers because they can become the face of the brand themselves.

But if you are not a famous person at the start, using your name may not be so recognizable to the majority of the people, so it will be harder, in the beginning, to try to make people aware of what your blog is all about, and what type of content you have in your blog.

Although, with the passage of time, when your readership widens, and you have more followers, you will become known and recognizable for your readers.

However, not all people who start a blog want to be known by their name. Some bloggers prefer to use a niche-specific naming convention and want to keep their identity separate from their blog's identity.

As mentioned earlier, if you choose to use your name as your brand, then it would be difficult for the readers to guess the niche of your blog. In case you select a name reflecting your niche, the readers will be able to instantly decide whether to read it or not.

Consistency In Using Your Brand Name In Other Online Platforms. Consistency is the key when you use your brand name across different social media. This will enable your followers to recognize you easily as the one and the same individual or entity and will help avoid confusion

There are many users who are accessing multiple platforms. They assume that since the brand name is same, the entity is owned by the same owners. In case, your website, blog, and social media pages are not named in the same manner, people will get confused, and you might lose some followers.

Protected Words. When you choose the name for your website or blog, you need to be careful as you don't want to select a name that is copyrighted, proprietary, or protected. You don't want to end up in trouble because of choosing such a name as it is legally forbidden. So you have to be aware of this stuff while brainstorming for a name for your blog.

Having A Domain Name For Your Blog

Your Blog's Domain Name Is Part Of Branding.

Consistency is of prime importance when you are trying to build a brand. The name of your blog is one of the elements of your blog's overall branding.

The domain name you choose is the first impression of your blog or business. A domain name is just as important as your blog's contents. Just like the logo of your brand, the name says a lot about it. It's a huge part of your identity and impacts your reputation.

Generic Domain Name and/or Blogspot URL Address

Sometimes, it is possible to get generic domain name for your blog. In that case, there is no need to register it or pay the registration fee.

Generic domain names are usually used when you use a free blogging platform and utilize their server to store all data pertaining to your blog for free.

There are specific formats for a generic domain name when you use Blogger.com or WordPress.com. Although you can utilize the generic names generated by these free sites for promoting your blog, the issue is that you don't have ownership of the selected domain name. If you want to switch the platform later on, you would not be able to carry the same name for your blog as it is specific to the free site you were using earlier.

Although you get to use such sites for free, I recommend not using a generic domain name. Firstly, it does not look professional when you use a generic domain name. People don't take those blogs seriously. Secondly, it is apparent that you are using the site for free, which does not carry a good message to your readers. Thirdly, a lot of your time and investment goes into promoting your blog. Let's suppose you need to switch the blogging platform later, then all your effort goes down the drain as you don't own the domain yourself.

Custom Domain Name

If you select a domain name for your blog and get it registered, then you have a custom domain name.

I recommend that you get the name registered through a registrar. It's always beneficial to have the same brand name as your blog's domain name or URL address.

First, check the availability of the name you have chosen. This can be done through a domain registration website or a registrar. If it's available, you can go ahead and register the name.

If you want to consider blogging in the long term, it's better to start exploring the process of selecting and registering the name as soon as possible. It will ensure help in building your brand from the onset. This will also minimize the risk that when later on you go to register the name, it's not even available.

If you don't plan to use a custom domain name in the long term, then you can simply keep using the generic domain name. It will help you save the registration fee and the hassle of registration.

Once your custom domain name is registered, you should start using it in all your promotions so that people start recognizing it since the beginning. You will be able to carry your domain name in the future, and thus, your marketing efforts would not be wasted due to the change of platform.

Let's suppose you delay having a custom domain name and build your audience using a generic domain name. In this scenario, when you customize your name, later on, all your initial efforts for building the audience would go to waste. You will have to build your brand all over again as the name is a significant part of your brand.

Sometimes, bloggers don't put effort into a customized domain or brand name because they don't expect to be hugely successful. However, they end up having a massive following. So, it is always better to sort out the issue of having a customized name in the beginning.

Although you might think it's too early for you to go into that hassle rather than focus on your blog writing, it is always recommended to sort these issues at the onset. This will help you a lot in the future. Also, the blogging world is changing so fast that you don't want someone grabbing your selected brand name before you go for registration.

Despite all the discussion above, I must say that it is not something imperative to have a custom domain name. It is neither required nor necessary. However, I want you to be aware of all possible scenarios that you might not be aware of in relation to your blogging journey.

Another aspect to consider is the cost of having a custom domain name. You will need to pay a yearly charge to the registrar should you choose to select a custom domain name. The cost varies from $10 to $35 per year. There is an additional privacy service available for an extra cost. It will restrict public display of your personal information as the owner of the domain name.

After knowing all these pros and cons, the final decision of whether to go for a custom domain name is all yours. It depends on the plans you have for your blog's future.

Comparison of Generic Domain Name and Custom Domain Name.

I personally think that the only cons of having a custom domain name are the process of registration and the yearly cost that you have to pay. However, the advantages outweigh the disadvantages. In any case, you have to invest a lot of time and effort and building your brand. So, if you have a custom domain name, you will reap the benefits in the long term.

The only situation in which your efforts will be wasted in case of owning a custom domain is if you decide to rebrand your whole online presence. In that case, you will have to begin from the very first step of choosing a new name and following the whole procedure of registering it and building your brand from there.

In more technical terms, changing your promoted custom domain name also means losing all the search engine rankings that your old domain name already achieved and losing all the backlinks that you already built over time.

Chapter 17

Email Marketing

If you talk to any successful blogger, they will tell you the importance of having an email list. Having someone's email will give you the power to contact them without hesitation. It is more likely for people to see and click on your email than it is for them to find out about your latest post online which means you cannot overlook the power of email and email marketing.

I will teach you how to collect emails through free traffic and pop-ups. Collecting emails can be a time-consuming and a laborious process, but very important.

I will do my best to make it simple for you. Remember that building a good email list will take time. Also, just because you have managed to collect 10,000 emails doesn't mean all of them will click on your email.

You need to make sure you are keeping your emails subscribers engaged and waiting for the next email, which we will teach you about in this chapter. Lastly, we will further guide you on how to create some of the most amazing emails. It will help you with getting a higher click-through rate. Even though email marketing is excellent, only 30% of people will read and click your email. You need to make all efforts to make sure they click on your email, and you need a well-written email.

Collecting Emails

When you start your blog, you won't have much money to spend on advertising. In this chapter, we will keep everything free, meaning, you won't have to pay a dime on collecting any emails. Now there are two main ways for you to obtain emails. The first one is through a pop-up.

You can use email resources like MailChimp to create a free pop up. What pop-up will help you with is when someone visits your website, they will get a big box right in front of them. It will ask them to sign up for our email list so they could get a free book or something along that line, as we talked about in the previous chapter. Depending on your niche, give your readers something of value.

If you're in the fitness Niche, you can offer your readers free eBooks on how to put on muscle, or if in the make money niche, maybe a guide on how to get started making money online? Figure out all the needs and problems people have in your niche. Create a free eBook or a cheat sheet and offer them for free. It is a must-have on your website. Chances are if people are on your site already, they won't hesitate to put their email in pop-ups for free information.

Landing page

Now the second way to collect emails would be to use something called a landing page. Once you sign up with mailchimp.com. which is free to use, you can then start creating free landing pages for your website. You can also use other pay monthly services for this such as Clickfunnels or Builderall, which come with multiple extra features perfect for your blogging needs. What a landing page will do is help you collect emails through YouTube and other sites. In the previous chapter, we talked about collecting emails through YouTube. This is where landing pages come in.

Make your landing page through mailchimp.com. Then copy that link and post it on your YouTube videos and other websites online. Your landing page will be offering a gift in exchange for their email. So if you go on to fitness forms and niche websites you can slowly add your landing page on there to specific people who are into your niche. It is also an excellent way for you to collect emails on your YouTube videos and other niche related websites. You need to have your landing page there up and running. If not, then you are missing out on a lot of free leads.

Creating email

Finally, the fun part, how to create an email and how often you should be sending emails to your readers. So the first thing you need to make sure is that you have your welcome email automated. If you're using the services, we recommend mailchimp.com. You should have no problem automating email because it is very straightforward.

Whenever someone signs up for your email list, the first thing you need to do is make sure you are sending them the gift you have promised. Your "welcome" email will be the only automated email, make sure your "welcome" email is sent immediately after they enter their email. This would be your automated email, now that you have created your welcome email and automated it, we will now talk about the frequency and the types of email you should be sending your subscribers.

Regarding sending rate, you should never email your readers more than four times a week. There are two reasons for it. First, you will have a lower chance of ending up in their spam email. Second, your readers won't get annoyed by your emails. Hence, they won't unsubscribe.

Regarding creating emails, update them about the latest blog and the affiliate products you want to offer them twice a week. This is a good rule of thumb I like to live by. Not only will they be engaged in the knowledge you provide them, but they will be likely to become your customers. It won't be like you're bombarded with sales pitch all the time. After trying this for years and years, I can tell you this is the best method of emailing your readers.

If you want to have a successful blog, you need to have your readers engaged through email. You can lose social media following, but the emails will live on forever. Some might consider email medieval, but most businesses are running solely on email marketing. Do not underestimate the power of email marketing, especially for bloggers. Use these methods we just talked about in this chapter to collect emails. Do not leave any stones unturned if you want to achieve success in blogging.

Chapter 18

THE PROS AND CONS OF BLOGGING

Still not convinced that blogging is right for you or you want to have all of the information before you make the decision to invest your time in doing something that you are still on the fence about.

Pros of Blogging:

- Actually starting your blog is easy. While it may not seem easy because you have to find the perfect topic to write about when you have gotten that out of the way, going to the blogging platform that you picked is going to be as simple as choosing a template and writing out your posts.
- If you have a website, then you are probably not adding a lot of new stuff that is keeping people coming back such as Facebook. So, a blog is going to be the perfect solution to get people to go to your website. If you really

want to make money with a blog, you are going to be adding new data to a blog on a constant basis. Therefore, more people are going to come to your blog. At the point in time that you have added new information to your website, then you are going to be able to let your blog readers know, and then, they are going to go to your website and be able to see what is new there. That way they are not constantly going to your website to see if there is any new information and finding nothing. This can become discouraging and be perceived as a waste of time.

- Having a blog can give you a sense of community. If you are someone who has social anxiety but does not want to be completely isolated or if you have an interest that makes it hard for you to find someone else to communicate within your immediate area, the blog is going to make it to where you are able to write out posts that require people to give you feedback through the responses that they generate. There is also the contact me option which is going to be the best way for people to get in touch with you one on one. Do not be afraid to put yourself out there; you already have a blog out there for you in the first place, so why hold back now?

- A blog is an excellent way to find sources of inspiration. You never know when you are going to need to look for something specific, and if you have a hard copy of it, then it is most likely going to get lost in the shuffle of daily life. So, instead, keep things that you want to look back on later on your blog! It is a lot easier for you to be able to do a search for the posts. Not to mention, if chosen appropriately, you are never going to have to clean out your archives, and you will have things for many years to come.
- You never know who you are going to be able to reach out to with your blog. Not every person that visits your blog is necessarily going to re-blog what you write, but there are going to be individuals who do, and that is going to cause an even bigger outreach.

Cons of blogging:

- While starting a blog is simple, it is going to take a lot of time and effort for you to keep it up. This means that you are going to have to post regularly to keep people coming back to read what it is that you write. This is when having a posting schedule is going to work out best for you because you can write posts days in advance and have them automatically post to your blog without you worrying about having to log in every day and figure out something to write.
- Although honesty is a good trait, too much of anything is bad. If you are too honest on your blog, then you are going to risk running off readers or clients. You need to think twice before you go and put something up on your blog because you never know who is going to know who or what you are talking about. While everyone wants to blow off steam, no one wants other people to know what they are talking about unless it is required that they are privy to the information that lets them know exactly what is going on. So, be careful about

what you are writing about! If you think that someone may figure out that you are writing about them, you may want to reconsider posting it.

- ➤ Your blog is a reflection of you. You are not going to want to have a blog that is known for spelling errors, straying off topic, and a design that does not make sense to its readers. Thus, make sure that your blog is an accurate representation of who you are and what you are representing. If you do not think that it is or you think that it is not getting any people to your blog, then you may want to consider changing the design and how you post things. In the event that your grammar and spelling are issues, there are free editors out there that will check that for you. Otherwise, you can pay for one and get everything checked so that it not only makes sense but is not plagiarized.
- ➤ Whenever something goes wrong with your blog, you are going to have to take the time to fix it or pay for someone to fix it for you. These unexpected technical issues are going to take time away from you getting people to

your blog as well as the time that you could spend writing on it. There are a number of technical issues that can go wrong with a blog, so you need to be sure that everything is up to date on your blog and that you are constantly having it checked for viruses.

Chapter 19

Avoiding Common Mistakes

Blogging, overall, is a relatively easy and fulfilling activity. But if you have your eyes set on creating a worthwhile blog, you need to make sure that you avoid the following steps:

Neglecting SEO

A lot of newbie bloggers tend to think that SEO is something they can work on later, and this is one of the biggest mistakes a blogger could ever consider making. SEO may not be your entire content marketing strategy, but it plays a significant role in getting your content out there. It's important that you take your keywords and content optimization strategies seriously from the get-go.

Remember, your content is going up against hundreds, if not thousands, of other blogs that are also in the same niche as yours. If you fail to optimize your content, your blog's reach will be heavily hindered. You need to take this seriously from the first moment.

By choosing to channel maximum energy into optimizing your content, you are giving yourself a greater advantage in the long run. For this to happen, you need to strategize and plan effectively. SEO and content optimization does not happen accidentally. It requires concentrated effort, and an eagerness to keep on trying until you finally find what works for you. This also requires patience.

Refusing to Interact with Other Bloggers

If you expect droves of followers to come your way and take in your content, without interacting with other bloggers and users on the scene, then you are not going to get very far. Blogging is a social activity – you need to put in as much effort as possible.

This effort shouldn't just be concentrated on creating great content; you also have to make room for networking. It's also important you realize that networking goes beyond liking another blogger's content and telling them to follow your blog. Reach out to them and find their social media platforms. You need to actually engage with other bloggers. Not only does it help you build your social profile as a blogger, but it also exposes you to what other people are writing.

Finding yourself among a circle of bloggers will help everyone in the long run; it may lead to new ways of promoting each other's content. As you grow with your blog, you will come to realize that blogging is more than just writing and uploading. If you really want a successful blog, you'll need to be willing to stretch yourself in many aspects.

Neglecting Social Media

Not only do you need to focus on fellow bloggers on the scene, but you also need to interact with your followers and subscribers. Social media is not for posting when you have a new post to put out there. The word "social" exists in social media for a reason. You have to engage with your followers. Engagement goes beyond asking a couple of questions related to your blog. Get to know your followers' interests and converse with them on that. Like and share their content too.

People respond well to bloggers and influencers who take an interest in what they have to offer. Your goal shouldn't be to just accumulate views and followers. Your goal should be to secure loyal subscribers who genuinely enjoy the content you have to share. The only place people are really going to understand who you are and what you have to offer is through social media. Social media platforms serve as a great place to speak your mind, share your thoughts, and also relate with other people who may have similar views to the ones you have.

Not Selecting a Niche

Some bloggers opt for being "general" instead of selecting a niche, and that often ends up being the major obstacle that stops them from succeeding as bloggers. You may have a lot of interests that you feel enthusiastic about sharing, but not all these interests need to feature on your blog. It's important that you find a niche to focus on. Otherwise, you'll fail to come up with a strategy that will effectively increase traffic and grow your reach. If your blog discusses automotive, gardening, and finances for example, how will you find a focus?

This is the reason why you must find a focus and work around it. That way you'll be able to create a blog that has an actual message. If you want to mention other topics of interest, you can feature them as special posts. But for the sole need for one to be able to monetize, and successfully build a blog, you need to select a niche. Selecting a niche will help you come up with diverse topics to talk on, in a focused manner.

All six of these steps are meant to help you create a blog that you can gain success from – even if you're just blogging for the fun of it. Blogging, when done right, can be one of the most fulfilling activities. If you do it right, you'll be able to make a significant amount of income from it – and who doesn't want that?

Chapter 20

How to Keep Your Traffic Coming Back?

Repurpose Old Content

One of the most important things you need to learn how to do as a blog owner is to repurpose your old content. Sometimes, even the most creative bloggers can have a hard time coming up with absolutely new material 100% of the time. You are not expected to do this, and in fact, it's even counterintuitive. Your readers keep coming back because they like what you have to say. You don't have to reinvent the wheel.

Make sure that you keep a pulse on your content and understand what has performed well and what hasn't. This is why having access to a program like Google Analytics is extremely important. Dig into your analytics and figure out which of your blog posts have performed extremely well and try to figure out why. Do you do best with topical subjects? Or is it your evergreen content that keeps people coming back?

"Evergreen content" is content that will stand the test of time and likely never go out of date. For example, an excellent recipe for your grandmother's chocolate cake is definitely evergreen content. Chocolate cake is not going to become outdated. On the other hand, a post about the very first Google Panda update is definitely topical and will become outdated. Anything regarding the apocalypse back in 2012 is also topical and is now considered outdated.

Content that is evergreen is very easily repurposed, as the information in it is still good. If you have a particular blog post that went viral and is evergreen, there's no reason not to recycle it. In terms of posts that are more topical, you may not be able to recycle the actual content of that blog, but you can take cues from the topic and the angle you took on it to help you create content that is along the same lines.

For example, an excellent way to repurpose "how to" topics in your blog is by taking a series of blog posts and turning them into a guide or eBook. If you had a lot of posts about Twitter advertising that did extremely well, consider taking all of those posts and compiling them into a book. You can then use the book on Amazon or use it as a freebie to entice people to sign up for your email marketing list.

Another excellent way to repurpose evergreen content is to turn it into an infographic. People love infographics; they are very easy and likely to be shared if they are done well. Of course, creating good infographics often requires a considerable amount of artistic skill.

Also, remember that you can repurpose your content to use directly on social media as well. For example, if you have a collection of interesting statistics, those make for fantastic twitter posts. Statistics are short and often entertaining. Using statistics from a blog post to create a Twitter post will help you increase your social media leverage.

Another creative way to recycle a good blog post is to consider starting a podcast channel. Many people prefer to listen to their blog post rather than actually read them. In this case, you can literally just read your blog post and not have to rewrite it at all. You may be surprised at the amount of attention you will get if you start a podcast channel. Again, people who sign up for your podcast may be inclined to sign up for your blog.

If you mostly work with PowerPoint presentations, those can easily be changed into SlideShare or YouTube posts. If you conduct webinars, those can also be converted into YouTube posts as well.

There are many clever and assorted ways to make use of your old content to keep on using excellent material that shouldn't be left out of the limelight simply because some time has passed! Bringing forward the content that brought your readers to your blog in the first place is an excellent idea to keep your blog fresh, interesting, and timeless.

Engage with Your Audience

We have spoken extensively about the importance of networking with other bloggers in your vertical.

However, if you want to keep your audience coming back for more time and time again, it is necessary to interact with them.

Remember that in the days of social media and instant communication, readers expect that their blog offers are going to take their concerns and considerations into account. They want to have a "live" experience with you, not have you be an unreachable author on a pedestal.

It is imperative to be around to answer questions on your blog. Again, this is a good way to make use of your analytics. Study the times of day when your blog gets the most traffic. This is a good time for you to post and then be around to interact with comments in real time if necessary. Anybody who comments on your blog should get a courteous and friendly response. Even if your response is mere "thanks!" this can make a world of difference.

Also, be open to friendly critique or suggestions. Especially if you are running your blog as a one-person operation, it will not be unusual for you to sometimes make typos or other small mistakes. If a commenter on your blog posts out grammatical or factual errors, make sure to thank them for their eagle eyes and then adjust your blog post accordingly with credit. People are more likely to come back to your blog and keep engaging with you if you create an environment of open conversation.

Social media is also extremely important in this. Many people who interact with you on social media will be your readers, not other bloggers. If one of your readers mentioned you in their social media, make sure to take the time to give them a shout out. On some social media platforms, you can even send private messages to people. This is a great way to personally thank individuals for interacting with your content and turn them into loyal readers.

Another way to encourage people to interact with your content is to offer contests or other fun activities. Many high-ranking brands use this to great aplomb, particularly on picture-heavy social media sites like Instagram. If people are participating in your contests with pictures, you can feature those pictures on your main social media platform, the more fun and interactive your brand persona is on social media, the more likely it is that people are going to follow you back and eventually find their way to your blog.

Another wonderful way to interact with your audience is to simply ask them what they want. In your blog, you can occasionally set up polls or other interactive devices to learn more about what your audience specifically wants to read about. People love to be asked their opinions; take advantage of this.

If you are a blogger who proves responsive, informative, and entertaining, people are going to keep coming back again and again. Remember that your content isn't just about the information that you spread; it is also about the person who is providing the content.

Chapter 21

Maintaining a Blog for Your Business

Creating a blog for your business is an excellent way to communicate with existing customers and also to strengthen the brand of your business. Unfortunately, most businesses believe maintaining a blog for their business is a time-consuming activity and requires a lot of effort. Due to this, they do not think that a blog can greatly benefit a business. So, you need to set aside such misconceptions and focus on creating a blog for your business, if you have one. It is necessary you realize maintaining a blog for your business is not a waste of time but a cost-efficient way to market your brand. In fact, businesses that have blogs which are regularly updated have found that they are able to generate three times as many leads as traditional outbound marketing. Promoting your business through blogs will ultimately lead to a boost in sales and broadening of your market. So, let's have a look at these tips before setting out to create a blog for your business, or if you have already started a business blog:

1. Write for the customers

As you have already learned, a business blog is different from a personal blog. People write personal blogs to attract readership, advertisements, or both. A business blog is not about attracting readership or advertisements; it is about your business and catering to the needs of your customers. When a person visits your blog, he or she is most likely an existing customer or a potential customer. So, you need to write the blog keeping your customers in mind. Your blog post should be informative and should be able to answer questions related to your business or service. Also, posts should be able to provide insight into your business or industry. Make a list of the things that customers constantly ask you in regards to your business. For instance, if you are a furniture making company that always has customers asking why you choose one type of wood over another, answering that question in a blog post is a great way to keep it geared at your customer.

2. Plan the content beforehand

As discussed in the previous chapters, you need to plan the content of your blog in advance. People in general enthusiastically start a blog for their business but fail to update it or add new content over time. The two most common reasons, or excuses, people give for not being able to add new content to their blog are:

- ❖ I just don't have the time!
- ❖ I can't think of anything new to write about!

Planning your blog in advance can solve these problems. With the right planning, as discussed in a previous chapter, there will be no shortage of time or ideas for your business blog. Planning the content for your blog will also help you to make sure that you are keeping your blog geared towards your audience and customers.

3. Write the content in a constructive manner

See that your blog offers quality information related to the business. Offering valuable information to the customers is the key to establish your business blog as a valuable source of information. For example, let's suppose you own a pet store that sells cats, dogs, their food, and accessories. Starting a blog is very advantageous for your business, and you can fill the blog with blog posts related to pets, pet foods, and accessories. You need to present the existing customers or prospective customers with information like how to choose the best foods for your pets, understanding the body language of your dog, different breeds of cats and dogs, the right way to hold a leash, how to deal with fleas, tips to travel with your cat, etc. If your customers receive valuable information through your blogs, they become more loyal in return.

4. See that posts are short and sweet

You should remember you are writing a blog post and not an essay. When people visit your blog, they don't go through your content word for word but tend to skim through the text to get an idea of what you have written in a particular post. So, a visitor will most likely read if the content is kept short, somewhere between 300 and 500 words. But, it is absolutely fine to use more words, up to 1500 if necessary, if your content demands it. Cover one topic at a time in your posts. It is better to have three articles that are 500 words a piece than it is to have one post that is 1500 words if you are writing about three different topics. If the topics are related, your readers can easily find them as the articles are linked together on your blog.

5. How often should you update your blog?

You need to stick to a schedule and be consistent in adding new content to your blog. Updating the blog once a week is a good practice. Pick a day of the week when you'd be free, like on weekends, and upload the new content. Google loves new content, so as you keep adding new content to your blog, its ranking increases.

6. See that responsibility is shared among team members

The responsibility of maintaining the blog shouldn't be the responsibility of a single team member. If that's the case, the person might become run out of ideas and become burdened by the responsibility. The best way to share responsibility is to rotate the blog among the members every month. When several people write on a single blog, more voices can be heard, and it gives more personality to the blog. Plus, if more people share the writing duty, the idea pool becomes larger, and the blog gets more and more innovative. If it is possible for your company, you can create a team that is responsible for your blog and leave it up to them to ensure that it is kept up to date. You can also have a place for all the people who work for your company to write down their ideas for your company blog. Keeping everyone involved helps to ensure that your blog will always have fresh ideas and will be a success.

7. Draw your inspiration from customers

Remember, you are primarily writing the blog for your customers. So, you need to research about what kind of questions your customers have in mind. It is not just enough if you answer those questions in an FAQ section; you need to answer them separately in blog posts. For example, the customers who bought pets at your pet store might have several questions regarding the food, accessories, and grooming of the pets. They would feel grateful if you could answer all those questions in a blog post dedicated to that purpose. Have your employees make lists of the most-commonly-asked questions. Also, ensure that you are advertising your blog to your customers as a way for them to have their questions answered by you. You don't want your blog to replace the expertise of your employees, but you do want people to be aware of how they can get answers from a trusted source, should they be unable to contact one of your employees.

8. Use the necessary imagery

Images often play an important role in turning potential readers into actual readers. You could provide them with imagery in the blog posts like infographics, behind the scene photographs, videos, graphs, etc. For example, you could post the pictures of different dogs available at your pet store and also behind the scene photographs of pets being fed and groomed in your store. Behind the scenes, pictures are often the most powerful for customers. They don't get to see the behind the scenes of your business, and when you give them that glimpse, they feel as though they are better able to trust you. You are showing your customers that you have nothing to hide and that you trust them with the information you are sharing. You could also provide them with graphs that illustrate the percentages of purchases of different kinds of dog breeds. If you were to use images from the Internet, be sure that they are under the Creative Commons license.

9. Respond to queries and complaints

Inviting customers to leave comments at the end of each blog is a good practice to encourage customers to interact with you. Most customers find it easy to post their queries through comments. So, keep an eye on the comments and make sure you respond to each and every one of them, especially the ones posted by existing customers. Also, if a customer criticizes your product or service in the comments, don't become impulsive and rudely reply to the comment. Always make sure your replies are polite, irrespective of whether the customer's comments have a positive or a negative tone. When a customer posts about a problem they had with a product or a representative of your company, don't just offer them false platitudes. Ensure that you take it as seriously as you would if that person was to walk into your store. Either give them your contact info so they can contact you to solve the problem or get their contact information so you can sort things out. When other readers see you do this, they are more likely to also have trust in your company because they can see that you care about your customers. This is also going to increase your business' number of customers.

Conclusion

Thank you for reading this guide. I hope it was informative and able to provide you with all of the tools you need to achieve your goals whatever it may be.

The next step is to use what you have learned in this book and put it to use! If you are just at the planning stage for your blog yet, then you are going to want to go out and start your blog first before you start trying to make money off of it.

Blogging, like anything else, is not easy when you first start out, but you will be able to master it sooner than you think you would. Just be patient and do not give up. Everything will fall into place as long as you are doing what you have been taught in this book.

Finally, if you found this book useful in any way, a review on Amazon is always appreciated!

Thank you and good luck!